Addiction Is a Choice

Addiction Is a Choice

Jeffrey A. Schaler, Ph.D.

OPEN COURT
Chicago and La Salle

To order books from Open Court, call toll-free 1-800-815-2280.

Cover illustration: © Kamil Vojnar, courtesy of Photonica, Inc.

Open Court Publishing Company is a division of Carus Publishing Company.

Library of Congress Cataloging-in-Publication Data

Schaler, Jeffrey A.
    Addiction is a choice / Jeffrey A. Schaler.
    p. cm.
    Includes bibliographical references and index.
    ISBN 0-8126-9403-1 (alk. paper). — ISBN 0-8126-9404-X (pbk. : alk. paper)
    1. Substance abuse. 2. Compulsive behavior. 3. Choice (Psychology) I. Title.
HV4998.S33 2000
    362.29—dc21   99-050090

To the memory of my father,
Otto Gerhard Julius Schaler,
who taught me about courage and vigilance;
and to my mother,
Elizabeth Schiltz Schaler,
who taught me about courage and forgiveness.

It is one of the most mysterious compensatory phenomena of our history that the individual, the more forcefully he seeks to emerge from a world rooted in collectivism, stubbornly undermines his own qualities, by means of a doctrine of man assigning each feature and peculiarity in turn to non-individual forces that in the end become completely dehumanized. . . . This is the alchemy of the modern age, the transmogrification of subject into object, of man into a thing against which the destructive urge may wreak its fury without restraint.

Alexander Mitscherlich and Fred Mielke,
Doctors of Infamy (1949)

Contents

About the Author

Jeffrey A. Schaler is a psychologist and consultant on addiction and social policy in Silver Spring, Maryland. He received his bachelor's degree in human interaction and group dynamics from Antioch College in 1973 and his master's degree (1986) and doctoral degree (1993) at the Institute for Child Study/Department of Human Development, University of Maryland College Park. He is an adjunct professor of justice, law, and society at American University's School of Public Affairs in Washington, D.C.; on the faculty teaching psychology at Johns Hopkins University; and an adjunct professor of psychology at Montgomery College in Rockville, Maryland. He served on the Montgomery County (Maryland) Drug Abuse Advisory Council from 1982 to 1988. A frequent guest over the years on national radio and television shows discussing addiction, psychiatry, law, and public policy, he edited *Drugs: Should We Legalize, Decriminalize, or Deregulate?* and co-edited, with Magda E. Schaler, *Smoking: Who Has the Right?*, both published in 1998. He lives in Erdenheim, Pennsylvania. His e-mail address is jschale@american.edu and his home page on the world wide web is at http://www.enabling.org/ia/szasz/schaler

Preface

Parts of this book are reworkings of material which first appeared in earlier writings of mine (see the Bibliography for full publication details): Schaler 1988a; 1989a; 1989c; 1989d; 1991; 1995a; 1995b; 1996a; 1996b; 1996d; 1997a, 1997b; 1997f; 1998b; 1998d.

My thinking about these and related matters is most strongly influenced by conversations over the years with Ron Aarons, Bruce K. Alexander, George J. Alexander, John O. Becker, Nelson Borelli, Ernest H. Bradley, Morris E. Chafetz, David J. Essex, Herbert Fingarette, Amos M. Gunsberg, Patrick Hickey, A. Tom Horvath, Nick Laird, Ron Leifer, John Marks, Paul Moore III, Christopher A. Rose, Martin W. Smith, Thomas S. Szasz, Arnold S. Trebach, and Richard Vatz. If you, reader, feel inclined to say 'that idea came from' any of those people it probably did.

I'm fortunate to have had the opportunity to teach thousands of students in diverse academic settings including American University, Johns Hopkins University, Montgomery College, and the Institute for Humane Studies at George Mason University—students who trusted, challenged, and respected me as we ventured together into so many new and difficult intellectual frontiers. In this regard, I would like to express a special appreciation for being invited to teach these and related ideas concerning mental illness, liberty, and justice at American University's School of Public Affairs for the past ten years. My academic freedom has always been supported there. I realize and appreciate now how rare academic freedom really is.

I would like to thank Mark Brady for inviting me to teach these and related ideas to students at the Institute for Humane Studies at George Mason University over the years.

Bruce Alexander, Patricia Erickson, and Michael Edelstein gave useful comments on parts of the manuscript.

Henry Azar and Alex W. Bauer kindly gave me important feedback on the history and science of nosology and pathology.

The conversations I've had with many hundreds of clients in my private practice over the past 26 years have been very important to my thinking on these and related matters. Thank you all for our work together.

A special thanks to Sunkyo Kwon in Berlin, Editor-in-Chief of *Psychnews International,* for giving me the opportunity to express many of my ideas and views on the Internet.

I'm also indebted to David Ramsay Steele, my editor at Open Court, for inviting me to write this book, as well as for his honesty, encouragement, and friendship.

My wife Renee and daughter Magda know more about my journey than anyone. I doubt I could have gotten here without them.

Introduction

They have addicted themselves to the ministry of the saints.

King James Bible, 1 Cor. xvi.15 (1611)

You Choose Your Addictions

'Addiction' is a fine old English word meaning commitment, dedication, devotion, inclination, bent, or attachment.

Particular addictions may be good or bad. Some folk are addicted to music, others to books, others to walks in the country. Some are addicted to a religious doctrine or community, be it the Roman Catholic, the Mormon, or the Zen Buddhist. Others are addicted to a political philosophy, like liberalism, socialism, or anarchism, or to a 'cause', like animal rights or free trade.

Some people are addicted to another person: perhaps their spouse, perhaps their latest flame. Others are addicted to a habit, like getting up early every morning. Michelangelo was addicted to painting and sculpting, Einstein was addicted to physics, Proust was addicted to writing, Gandhi was addicted to independence for India. Many others, of course, have been equally addicted to these pursuits, but have lacked exceptional talent.

Sometimes addictions fade gradually. The ardent lover becomes the jaded husband, or the heavy drinker of alcohol gradually moderates. Other times, one addiction is suddenly replaced by another: the ardent lover of x becomes the ardent lover of y, or the heavy drinker becomes instead a born-again Christian. Malcolm X relates how converts to the Nation of Islam quickly abandoned any of their former drug-taking habits.

An addiction is not exactly the same as a habit, though one can be addicted *to* a habit. John Stuart Mill refers to "A man who causes grief to his family by addiction to bad habits." Addiction is a fondness for, or orientation toward, some thing or activity, because it has meaning, because it is considered valuable or even sacred. In some cases, people may be addicted to something because they find it enjoyable, and this, of course, also reflects their values: such a person believes that the right way to live is to seek enjoyment.

Human life is always involved with addictions, and would be wretched and worthless, perhaps even impossible, without addictions. *Addico, ergo sum.* Yet human life can be devastated or horribly blighted by ill-chosen addictions. A simple example would be that of an adolescent drawn into an apparently warm and benevolent religious group, which only gradually comes forth in its true colors as a destructive cult of collective suicide. Another example might be a young person in the 1930s, becoming a Communist or a National Socialist.

Addictions are indispensable. Addictions—and only addictions—can open us up to all that makes life rich and fulfilling. Yet addictions can also have appalling consequences. The conclusion is clear: choose your addictions very carefully! Nothing is more vital for a young person than to select the right addictions. Addictions we approve of are called 'virtues'. Addictions we disapprove of are called 'vices'.

Can Addiction Be Involuntary?

In recent years, the word 'addiction' has come to be used with quite a different meaning. It is now taken to refer to any activity which individuals engage in, deliberately and consciously, and are *physically unable* to stop themselves pursuing. Thus (it is claimed) the heroin addict cannot refrain from injecting himself with heroin, the alcohol addict or 'alcoholic' cannot refrain from swallowing alcoholic beverages, Bill Clinton cannot refrain from having sexual relations with his subordinates, the overspending housewife cannot refrain from buying 'unnecessary' things in stores, and the compulsive gambler cannot stop gambling.

In this newfangled sense of 'addiction', I maintain that 'addiction' is a myth. I deny that there is any such thing as 'addiction', in the sense of a deliberate and conscious course of action which the person literally cannot stop doing. According to my view of the world, the heroin addict can stop injecting himself with heroin, the alcohol addict can stop himself from swallowing whiskey, and so forth. People are responsible for their deliberate and conscious behavior.

I find it difficult to avoid smiling while solemnly stating the above, since it's so manifestly true. Most people are tacitly aware that it's true, regardless of what the pundits tell them. But leading 'authorities'—usually journalists who know nothing—keep on telling the public that 'addicts' *physically cannot stop doing* whatever it is that they do (and the authority objects to them doing).

As a simple and ludicrous example, take the campaign against smoking tobacco. We are constantly being told that cigarettes are addictive, and that this means that teenagers who start smoking will be 'hooked' for life.

Meanwhile, millions of heavy, habitual, lifelong cigarette smokers have quit smoking, the vast majority of them without any professional help or 'treatment'. Inescapably, for these millions of smokers, smoking was a choice—was presumably *always* a choice, even during the decades when they were smoking every day. How do the proponents of the 'involuntary addiction' ideology respond to this evidence? Amazingly, they claim that, while those smokers who chose to quit were indeed able to make that choice, exactly those smokers who have not so far quit smoking are unable to do so! Notice that according to this way of thinking, individuals demonstrate their inability to make a choice simply by making the 'wrong' choice, the one we wish they hadn't made.

In the pursuit of such ideological campaigns, any absurdity will be accepted. For example, what is it that smokers are addicted to? Nicotine, say the anti-smoking fanatics. But there are many ways to get nicotine into one's body: injection, swallowing tablets, a skin patch, and so forth. The vast majority of the injurious health effects attributed to smoking (such as lung cancer) have nothing to do with nicotine. The fear of lung cancer has induced millions of individuals to give up smoking cigarettes, but it has induced very few to start swallowing nicotine tablets. Evidently, we are witnessing confusion and incoherence, even at the most elementary level.

"Those who believe absurdities will commit atrocities," said Voltaire. Pointing out such simple blunders as those mentioned above will not always be immediately effective in persuading the anti-smoking crusaders to abandon their illiberal and monstrous campaign of repression. They are *addicted* to their anti-smoking bigotry. Their addiction does not relieve them of responsibility for their actions. We are all responsible for our addictions and for the actions we perform in pursuit of our addictions. The anti-smoking bigots have chosen their addiction—a particularly nasty one whose ill-effects fall mainly on other people, not themselves. They are addicted to the notion that the police should chase people who live incorrectly, forcing them to comply with the currently fashionable definition of a wholesome lifestyle. The same goes for all those who wage a *war on people*, calling it a 'war on drugs'.

Changing One's Addictions May Be Hard

It is often not a simple matter to induce people to give up their vicious addictions and replace them with virtuous ones. Their values, the principles that give meaning to their lives, need to be transformed. They may not share our opinion as to which addictions are virtuous and which addictions are vicious. But even if they do share our opinion, in the sense that they assent to it, they may hold other beliefs which imply a continued commitment, that is, a continued addiction, to the old way of life. The transition from one addiction to a different addiction—from drunkenness to sobriety, from sexual promiscuity to marital fidelity, from frequenting the local casino to frequenting the local Episcopalian church—may be a difficult struggle.

A person with an addiction may come to believe that this addiction is not really for the best. That person may decide it would be better to abandon it. But because all our beliefs, values, habits, and physiological responses are an intricately woven web, that person may often find the 'tug' of their old addiction quite powerful. Turning away from the thing which has been the pivot on which one's existence has turned, the altar at which one has worshiped daily, the central activity of one's life, may take effort and application. It may not be as easy as snapping one's fingers. There is no need to dream up some far-fetched, scientifically worthless fantasy about 'physical addiction' to account for this fact, familiar as it has been down the ages. Or do we really suppose that a nineteenth-century African villager, converted to Christianity by white missionaries, a villager who then suffered the most agonizing terrors because he was no longer performing the rituals required to placate the animistic spirits of his traditional culture, was suffering from a medical condition, physical dependence upon animistic religion?

In saying that addiction is a choice, I don't mean to imply that it is always an *easy* choice. I don't deny that people have problems, and among these problems may be attachments which are difficult to break off, undesirable habits that are hard to shake. 'Breaking up is so very hard to do', says the old pop song. It's true of practices as well as people.

I do not, of course, dispute that many people are properly objects of our compassion and help because they feel that their lives are out of control. Indeed, I have spent much of my working life as a psychologist trying to help such people. I have often found, however, that a person suffering from a harmful addiction ('presenting with' it, as we psychologists like to say), whether to the ingestion of a chemical substance or to some other pattern of behavior, actually has a different problem in his or her life, a problem not obviously related to the addiction. When that problem is resolved, I often find that the person abandons the harmful addiction.

It's ironic that the ideologues of 'involuntary addiction' make it more difficult to help such people. They do this by preaching that addiction to the practice of consuming a chemical substance, such as alcohol or cocaine, is a disease. Their first job, they believe, is to convince 'addicts' that they are sick, and therefore not responsible for their actions. In my judgment, this is just about the worst thing we could possibly tell such people. To someone engaged in a bitter struggle to give up one way of life and find a replacement, it is discouraging and demoralizing to be informed that their old way of life is somehow fated, predetermined by their body chemistry. It's also untrue. I always advise such individuals that they can control themselves and their lives, that they have the power to renounce an old addiction, if they really want to. This, I believe, is helpful to them. It's also the truth.

In this book, I sometimes compare drug addiction with religion. Religious devotion or piety is one of the most familiar addictions. Another is romantic love, the addiction to another specific individual, a potential sexual partner. I do not make these comparisons to demean religion or love, or to defend drug addiction. I merely seek to accentuate an underlying similarity.

Though drawing attention to parallels among different addictions, I don't maintain that all addictions are on a par. When it comes to the consumption of chemical substances, I like a glass or two of wine or scotch, and occasionally more than two. I also sometimes, usually earlier in the day, like a cup or two of good strong coffee. I don't consume heroin, cocaine, or tobacco, and if asked for my advice, I generally recommend against consuming those substances. On the other hand, I utterly oppose the government's 'war' against the people who consume or provide these substances. If asked for advice, I would also recommend against joining the Moonies, Transcendental Meditation, or Scientology—or, for that matter, a purportedly therapeutic religious cult like Alcoholics Anonymous. And similarly, I completely oppose government persecution of these cults.

Since there is an underlying similarity between addiction to religion and addiction to drug-taking, I favor extending the First Amendment 'establishment' and 'free exercise' clauses to drug-taking. It is no more the business of the government what chemical substances you put into your body than it is the government's business where or in what manner you practice your religion. Following a remark often attributed to Voltaire, I disagree with what you say, but I will defend to the death your right to say it. Following Thomas Szasz, I disagree with the drug you take, but I will defend to the death your right to take it.

Two Ways of Looking at Addiction

We be virgins, and addicted to virginity.
Robert Greene, *Arcadia* (1590)

Today, just about everyone believes, or says they believe, that addicts—including regular smokers, heavy drinkers, frequent gamblers, presidents who seduce interns, and people who run up credit card debts—can't help themselves. They are driven by an irresistible compulsion, and this compulsion is allegedly a medically recognized disease, which can be treated.

"Just about everyone" includes politicians, government officials, social workers, addiction treatment providers, physicians, ministers of religion, and the media. There is, however, one exception: those people who actually know something about the subject. These are the psychologists, physicians, and social scientists who have researched addiction, and those others who have closely followed their findings and the ensuing scholarly debates. These people are divided on the issue; their views are more diverse than those of the politicians and media, and it is fair to say that many of them are increasingly skeptical of the disease model. As we shall see, the results of research on addiction certainly do not bear out the disease theory, and are actually hard to reconcile with it.

1

I should add that although "just about everyone," with the exception of those who know something about addiction, *appears* to swallow the disease theory, with many people this acceptance does not go very deep. They generally hold conflicting and contradictory views, in which assent to the disease model is combined with a disregard for it in practice.

A little over two hundred years ago, the disease model was completely unknown, as it had been throughout history up to that point. No one, for example, thought that habitual drunkenness was due to a disease (though many knew it could *cause* diseases—a very different matter). The tremendous sea-change in opinion which led to the present dominance of the disease model did not result from new scientific findings. No scientist or physician has ever 'discovered' the disease of addiction! As a matter of historical fact, the disease model did not originate with scientific research. It emanated, in the first instance, from religious thinking about social problems, especially from the form of Protestantism associated with the nineteenth-century Temperance movement.

The Disease Model—What It Is

According to the disease model, what does 'addiction' mean? Let's look at some typical formulations. Psychologist James R. Milam and writer Katherine Ketcham, authors of *Under the Influence*, are popular spokespersons for the disease-model camp. They contend that alcoholics should not be held accountable for their actions because these are the "outpourings of a sick brain. . . They are sick, unable to think rationally, and incapable of giving up alcohol by themselves" (Milam and Ketcham 1983).

Similarly, physician Mark S. Gold, considered an expert on cocaine use and treatment, says in his book *800-Cocaine* that cocaine should not be regarded as a benign recreational drug, because it can cause addiction. As with alcoholism, says Gold, the only 'cure' for cocaine addiction involves permanent and total abstention from its use. Cocaine purportedly produces "an irresistible compulsion to use the drug at increasing doses and frequencing in the face of serious physical and/or psychological side effects and the extreme disruption of the user's personal relationships and system of values" (Gold 1985). According to Gold "If you feel addicted, you are addicted." I doubt that he would accept that if you don't feel addicted, you're not addicted. In view of the frequent claim that addiction is a disease 'just like diabetes', try this on for size: 'If you feel diabetic, you are diabetic.'

The former National Drug Policy Director William J. Bennett has explained (in a 1989 speech in San Diego) that an addict "is a man or woman whose power to exercise . . . rational volition has . . . been seriously eroded by drugs, and whose life is instead organized largely—even exclusively—around the pursuit and satisfaction of his addiction." One might, of course, wonder how someone whose power to exercise rational volition has been badly damaged can be so effective at organizing his life around his addiction. An act of organizing is clearly a volitional act, the exercise of will. And all the more so if there are many successive acts of organizing, unified by a common purpose.

Celebrities often make a public confession of their drug addiction and claim that they cannot be held responsible for it, or for assorted criminal acts they performed while addicted. Typical is Marion Barry's assertion, when he was 54 and mayor of the District of Columbia: "That was the disease talking . . . I was a victim."

Fourteen charges were lodged against Barry by the U.S. Attorney's office, including three counts of perjury, a felony offense for lying about drug use before a grand jury; ten counts of cocaine possession, a misdemeanor; and one count of conspiracy to possess cocaine. Barry considered legal sanctuary, but settled for moral sanctuary, in what has come to be known as the disease-model defense. He maintained that he was "addicted to alcohol and had a chemical dependency on Valium and Xanax." These are diseases, he explained, "similar to cancer, heart disease and diabetes." The implication: it is as unfair to hold him responsible for drug-related criminal behavior as it is to hold a person who has diabetes responsible for their abnormal blood sugar levels.

The suggestion was that Barry's disease of addiction forced him to use drugs, which in turn eroded his volition and judgment. He did not voluntarily or willfully break the law. According to Barry, "the best defense to a lie is truth," and the truth, he contended, is that he was powerless in relation to drugs, his life allegedly unmanageable and "out of control."

Barry's actions were purportedly symptomatic of his disease. And jail, say those who agree with him, is not the answer to the "product of an illness." I agree, on entirely different grounds, that no one should be jailed for using or possessing cocaine or other drugs. Unfortunately most people who oppose the jailing of drug consumers usually go on to demand even more lavish government spending on 'treatment'. This is wrong-headed for a number of reasons, the simplest being that *addiction treatments don't work.*

After his arrest at the Vista Hotel in Washington, D.C., Marion Barry went through treatment for alcohol addiction and chemical dependency at the Hanley-Hazelden clinic in West Palm Beach, Florida, and at the Fenwick Hall facility near Charleston, South Carolina. Barry said he needed treatment because he had "not been spiritual enough." His plan was to turn his "entire will and life over to the care of God . . . using the Twelve-Step method and consulting with treatment specialists." He said he would then "become more balanced and a better person."

The Twelve-Step program Barry attempted to follow was developed by Alcoholics Anonymous (AA), a spiritual self-help fellowship with specific religious views. AA and its offspring Narcotics Anonymous (NA) are the major methods of dealing with alcoholism and addiction today. All 'good' addiction treatment facilities and treatment programs aim at getting their 'patients' into AA and similar programs such as NA.

Yet several courts throughout the United States, in cases involving First Amendment violations, have determined that AA is a religion and not a form of medicine. Anthropologist Paul Antze has written extensively on AA and describes the "point-by-point homology between AA's dramatic model of the alcoholic's predicament and the venerable Protestant drama of sin and salvation."

What kind of 'disease' is it for which the most popular and prestigious 'treatment' is a conversion experience in a religious cult?

The Credo of the Disease Model

Let's now set out the main tenets of disease-model thinking. These were developed mainly in application to alcohol addiction ('alcoholism') but are usually now extended to all substance addictions.

1. Most addicts (alcoholics) don't know they have a problem and must be forced to recognize they are addicts (alcoholics).

2. Addicts (alcoholics) cannot control themselves when they take drugs (drink alcoholic beverages).

3. The only solution to drug addiction (alcoholism) is treatment.

4. Addiction (alcoholism) is an all-or-nothing disease: A person cannot be a temporary drug addict (alcoholic) with a mild drug (drinking) problem.

5. The most important step in overcoming addiction (alcoholism) is to acknowledge that you are powerless and can't control it.

6. Complete abstinence, not moderation, is the only way to control drug addiction (alcoholism).

7. Physiology alone, not psychology, determines whether one person will become drug-addicted (alcoholic) and another will not.

8. The fact that addiction (alcoholism) runs in families means that it is a genetic disease.

9. People who are drug-addicted (alcoholics) can never outgrow addiction (alcoholism) and are always in danger of relapsing.

Good and Bad Addictions

In its traditional definition, addiction simply means that someone likes to do something, moves toward something, or says yes to something. As Alexander and Schweighofer (1988) have pointed out, addiction can be 'positive' (good) or 'negative' (bad), drug- or non-drug related, and characterized by tolerance and withdrawal or not characterized by tolerance and withdrawal.

Tolerance refers to the fact that through continued use of a drug, or repetition of some activity, people often feel the need to 'increase the dose' to produce the kind of pleasurable experience they once had. *Withdrawal* refers to the physiological (as well as psychological) changes that occur when drug use ceases.

A positive addiction enhances the values we hold dear. Through a positive addiction we pull our life together, creating meaning and purpose. Obviously, that sense of meaning and purpose varies from person to person. A negative addiction pulls our life apart. By engaging in a negative addiction we live in conflict with ourselves, which again bears on the sense of meaning and purpose in our lives. Positive addictions may include alcohol, work, and love. Negative addictions may also include alcohol, work, and love. Addictions are as diverse as peoples' values.

The newer usage of 'addiction' to refer to drugs, loss of control, withdrawal, and tolerance, along with the theory that addiction is a disease, developed out of the moralistic rhetoric of the temperance and anti-opium movements of the nineteenth century. This restricted use of the word served several purposes, according to Alexander and Schweighofer. It was a trend of the times to medicalize social deviancy—to label those who contravened society's norms as sick and in need of treatment. Linking addiction to drugs and illness suggested it was a medical problem. This link could also be employed in an attempt to scare people away from drug use, a tactic that became increasingly important to anti-opium reformers. In its origin, the anti-opium movement was a racist anti-immigration movement, directed against West Coast Chinese, who were thought to be able to work harder because of opium and thus unfairly undercut the working conditions of Caucasian laborers.

Consider one of the most uncomfortable and difficult addictions we know of. This addiction can be either positive or negative, depending on many circumstances. It is characterized by both tolerance and withdrawal: the emotional and physical manifestations of withdrawal are frequently severe (they can be far more severe than is usually the case with heroin or cocaine). These pangs of withdrawal often lead to suicide, and withdrawal from this addiction is indeed a major cause of death among young people. The addiction is called 'love'.

On the other hand, many other people use allegedly addicting drugs (pursue romantic relationships) for long periods of time, choose to give up those drugs (love objects), and then experience virtually no symptoms of tolerance or withdrawal, let alone irresistible cravings causing them to continue to use drugs (seek out the loved one) at any expense.

The Iron Will of the Addict

The disease model credo dominates present-day drug policy. Yet some of its tenets are rejected by the great majority of addiction researchers. Taken as a package, these beliefs are somewhat contradictory: the thinking and motivation of the addict are considered to be, at the same time, both absolutely crucial and totally immaterial. Addiction is a 'disease' to be 'treated', yet 'treatment' consists of talking sessions aimed at changing the addict's beliefs and motives.

Disease-model advocates maintain that addiction cannot be controlled through an act of will: the heavy drinker or drug user has an 'impaired will'. Addiction is characterized by an inability willfully to control one's behavior, especially in relation to certain kinds of 'addictive' drugs, for example, alcohol, heroin, cocaine, or nicotine.

The opposite view is surely worth considering. Heavy drinking and drug use are characterized by strong will. The more single-mindedly self-destructive the drinker or other drug user is, the more indicative their behavior is of a strong will, even an iron will. If the term *addict* has come to imply passivity and involuntariness, a more accurate word (from the same Latin root) to describe the person who chooses a negative addiction is *dictator*. These people become dictators, of a sort, by choosing to consume alcohol and other 'addictive' drugs, possibly at the expense of family, job, and health, making themselves and other people suffer from their iron will.

Some other 'dictators' do the same with chess, body-building, money-making, music, ministering to the poor, or pursuing enlightenment. We often tend to applaud those who ruthlessly subordinate their lives to an over-riding purpose we consider valuable; we often tend to boo and hiss those who ruthlessly subordinate their lives to an over-riding purpose we consider pointless or destructive. Considered in this way, addiction becomes an ethical issue.

When drug-addicted dictators turn away from alcohol through disease-model-based treatment programs such as AA, their iron will may become an iron fist. They then demand that others *abdicate* to their definitions of addiction as a disease. In other words, their dictatorship comes first no matter how or where they impose it.

Self-Efficacy versus the Disease Model

An important concept in contemporary psychology is self-efficacy. Technically, self-efficacy is people's confidence in their ability to achieve a specific goal in a specific situation. It refers to the capability people believe they possess to effect a specific behavior or to accomplish a certain level of performance. Self-efficacy is not the skills one has but rather one's judgment of what one can do with those skills (Bandura 1977; 1986).

You do not need psychologists to know that having confidence in your ability to achieve something for yourself has a lot to do with whether you will actually make the effort to succeed at something you set your mind to do. While self-efficacy is a scientific concept, tested by psychologists in various settings, it's also common sense. When you believe you can do something, you are more likely to be successful at it. When you believe you cannot do something, you are more likely to be unsuccessful at it. We tend to try to do what we believe we can do. We tend not to try to do what we believe we cannot do.

For those of us who favor the development of self-efficacy in individuals, who prefer to see people in charge of their own lives, the message taught by the disease model is profoundly discouraging.

The Free-Will Model: What It Is

According to those who reject the disease model, humans are capable of deliberate action in pursuit of chosen goals. Although much human behavior is not carefully thought out, the acting person may at any moment pay more attention to such thoughtless behavior, and consciously modify it. All such voluntary human action is ultimately under conscious control, and is to be distinguished from an unconscious reflex or seizure, which is involuntary.

Whenever we see someone behaving in a conscious, goal-directed manner (rushing to get to the liquor store before it closes, laying in a supply of alka seltzer, and so forth) we can be sure that this behavior is not to be explained by physiology alone. Physiology alone can never determine that someone will take a drug, or how often they will take it. Part of their motivation may be to make themselves feel better, and the explanation for this may owe something to physiology. But their beliefs, values, and goals are also essential in forming their intentions.

Heavy, habitual users of drugs, including alcohol, often moderate or cease taking the drug without help from anyone else. There is no evidence that any form of 'addiction treatment' can increase the proportion of drug consumers who moderate or halt their consumption of drugs.

Individuals in the habit of taking a drug frequently or heavily may, and often do, decide to moderate or to quit. If they decide to quit, they may decide to stop suddenly or to taper off gradually. No one technique is best for everyone. Some people will be happiest reducing their intake to a modest level, others will wish to quit completely. Of the latter, some will be happiest quitting abruptly, others will prefer to gradually taper off. The notion that 'once you're an addict, you're always an addict', that an addict (or alcoholic) can never be cured but only 'in remission', is nothing but religious dogma; it does not have a shred of scientific support.

The Credo of the Free-Will Model

1. The best way to overcome addiction is to rely on your own willpower. (*You* are the 'higher power'.)
2. People can stop depending on drugs or alcohol as they develop other ways to deal with life.
3. Addiction has more to do with the environments people live in than with the drugs they are addicted to.
4. People often outgrow drug and alcohol addiction.
5. Alcoholics and drug addicts can learn to moderate their drinking or cut down on their drug use.
6. People become addicted to alcohol and other drugs when life is going badly for them.
7. Drug addicts and alcoholics can and often do find their own ways out of their addictions, without outside help.
8. You have to rely on yourself to overcome an addiction.
9. Drug addiction is often a way of life people rely on to cope with, or avoid coping with, the world.

If you find these propositions ludicrous or outrageous, you are addicted to the disease model. I hope to persuade you to addict yourself to the truth. Switching addictions is rarely easy or painless. It takes the exercise of willpower, but you do have plenty of that.

2

Is Addiction Really a Disease?

Being addicted to a melancholy as she is.

William Shakespeare, *Twelfth Night*

If you watch TV, read the newspaper, or listen to almost any social worker or religious minister, you soon pick up the idea that addiction is a condition in which addicts just physically cannot control themselves, and that this condition is a medical disease.

The federal government views alcohol addiction as a disease characterized by *loss of control*, with a physiological 'etiology' (cause) independent of volition. According to a typical statement of the government's view by Otis R. Bowen, former secretary of health and human services,

> millions of children have a genetic predisposition to alcoholism . . . alcohol use by young people has been found to be a 'gateway' drug preceding other drug use . . . about 1 out of every 15 kids will eventually become an alcoholic. . . . alcoholism is a disease, and this disease is highly treatable. (Bowen 1988, pp. 559, 563)

You may easily conclude that all the experts agree with this kind of thinking. Most people with no special interest in the subject probably never get to hear another point of view.

11

The true situation is a bit more complicated. Public opinion overwhelmingly accepts the claim that addiction is a disease, but the general public's views are seriously inconsistent. A 1987 study of public views on alcoholism showed that over 85 percent of people believe that alcoholism is a disease, but most of them also believe things that contradict the disease theory. Many people seem to support and reject the disease theory at the same time. For instance, they often say they believe that alcoholism is a disease and also that it is a sign of moral weakness (Caetano 1987, p. 158).

The addiction treatment providers, the many thousands of people who make their living in the addiction treatment industry, mostly accept the disease theory. They are, in fact, for the most part, 'recovered addicts' themselves, redeemed sinners who spend their lives being paid to preach the gospel that social deviants are sick.

Among those psychologists and others who think, write, discuss, and conduct research in this area, however, opinion is much more divided. In this small world, there is an ongoing battle between the 'disease model' and the 'free-will model'.

Biomedical and psychosocial scientists range across both sides of the controversy (Fillmore and Sigvardsson 1988). Some biomedical researchers accept the disease model and assert that genetic and physiological differences account for alcoholism (for example, D.W. Goodwin 1988; F.K. Goodwin 1988; Blum et al. 1990; Tabakoff and Hoffman 1988). Other biomedical researchers have investigated their claims and pronounced them invalid (Lester 1989; Bolos et al. 1990; Billings 1990). Many social scientists reject the idea that alcoholics or other addicts constitute a homogeneous group. They hold that individual differences, personal values, expectations, and environmental factors are key correlates to heavy drinking and drug-taking. Others reject strictly psychological theories (Maltzman 1991; Madsen 1989; Vaillant 1983; Milam and Ketcham 1983; Prince, Glatt, and Pullar-Strecker 1966). Some sociologists regard the disease model of alcoholism as a human construction based on desire for social control (Room 1983; Fillmore 1988). Some embrace the disease model even while agreeing that addiction may not be a real disease—they hold that utility warrants labeling it as such (Kissin 1983; Vaillant 1990). Their opponents believe the disease model does more harm than good (Szasz 1972; Fingarette 1988; Alexander 1990a; 1990b; Crawford et al. 1989; Fillmore and Kelso 1987; Heather, Winton, and Rollnick 1982; Schaler 1996b).

My impression is that the disease model is steadily losing ground. It may not be too much to hope that the notion of addiction as a disease will be completely discredited and abandoned in years to come, perhaps as early as the next 20 years.

If this seems like a fanciful speculation, remember that other recognized 'diseases' have been quite swiftly discredited. The most recent example is homosexuality. Being sexually attracted to members of one's own sex was, overwhelmingly, considered a disease by the psychiatric profession, and therefore by the medical profession as a whole, until the 1960s. Psychiatry and medicine completely reversed themselves on this issue within a few years. Homosexuality was declassified as an illness by the American Psychiatric Association in 1973. It is now officially considered a non-disease, unless the homosexual wishes he were not a homosexual. This doesn't go far enough, but imagine the same principle extended to drug addiction: the addict is not at all sick unless he says he is unhappy being addicted!

Before homosexuality, there were the recognized diseases of masturbation, negritude (having a black skin), Judaism (described as a disease by the German government in the 1930s), and being critical of the Soviet government, which 'treated' political dissidents in mental hospitals (see Rush 1799; Szasz 1970; Robitscher 1980; Lifton 1986; Conrad and Schneider 1992; and Breggin 1993). A similar fate may be in store for the 'disease' of drug addiction.

Many people accept the disease model of addiction on the basis of respect for the messenger. Addiction is a disease because doctors say it's a disease (social psychologists call this peripheral-route processing) rather than critical evaluation of the message itself (central-route processing). Peripheral-route processing has more in common with faith than reason, and research shows that in general its appeal is greatest among the less educated. Reason and faith are not always compatible. Reason requires evidence, faith does not.

Clinical and public policy should not be based on faith, whether the source is drunken anecdote, the proclamations of self-assigned experts, or the measured statements of addiction doctors. Rather, empirical evidence and sound reasoning are required. Both are lacking in the assertion that addiction is a disease.

If it were ever to be shown that there existed a genetic disease causing a powerful craving for a drug, this would not demonstrate that the afflicted person had no choice as to whether to take the drug.

Nor would it show that the action of taking the drug was itself a disease.

There are various skin rashes, for example, which often arouse a powerful urge to scratch the inflamed area. It's usually enough to explain the harmful consequences of scratching, and the patient will choose not to scratch. Though scratching may cause diseases (by promoting infection of the area) and is a response to physiological sensations, the activity of scratching is not itself considered a disease.

What Is a Disease?

Is addiction really a disease? Let's clarify a few matters. The classification of behavior as socially unacceptable does not prove its label as a disease. Adherents of the disease model sometimes respond to the claim that addiction is not a disease by emphasizing the terrible problems people create as a result of their addictions, but that is entirely beside the point. The fact that some behavior has horrible consequences does not show that it's a disease.

The 'success' of 'treatment programs' run by people who view addiction as a disease would not demonstrate that addiction was a disease—any more than the success of other religious groups in converting people from vicious practices would prove the theological tenets of these religious groups. However, this possibility need not concern us, since all known treatment programs are, in fact, ineffective.

I will not go into the claims of a genetic basis for 'alcoholism' or other addictions. A genetic predisposition toward some kind of behavior, say, speaking in tongues, would not show that those with the predisposition had a disease. Variations in skin and eye color, for example, are genetically determined, but are not diseases. Fair-skinned people sunburn easily. The fairness of their skin is genetically determined, yet their susceptibility to sunburn is not considered a disease. Neither would a genetic predisposition toward some kind of behavior necessarily show that the predisposed persons could not consciously change their behavior.

With so much commonsense evidence to refute it, why is the view of drug addiction as a disease so prevalent? Incredible as it may seem, because doctors say so. A leading alcoholism researcher once asserted that alcoholism is a disease simply because people go to doctors for it. Undoubtedly, drug 'addicts' seek help from doctors for two reasons. Many addicts have a significant psychological investment in maintaining this view, having been told, and come to believe, that their eventual recovery depends on believing they have a disease. They may even have come to accept that they will die if they question the disease model of addiction. And treatment professionals have a significant economic investment at stake. The more behaviors are diagnosed as diseases, the more they will be paid by health insurance companies for 'treating' these diseases.

When we consider whether drug addiction is a disease we are concerned with what causes the drug to get *into* the body. It's quite irrelevant what the drug does *after* it's in the body. I certainly don't for a moment doubt that the taking of many drugs *causes* disease. Prolonged heavy drinking of alcoholic beverages can cause cirrhosis of the liver. Prolonged smoking of cigarettes somewhat raises the risk of various diseases such as lung cancer. But this uncontroversial fact is quite distinct from any claim that the activity is itself a disease (Szasz 1989b).

Some doctors make a specialty of occupation-linked disorders. For example, there is a pattern of lung and other diseases associated with working down a coal mine. But this does not show that mining coal is itself a disease. Other enterprising physicians specialize in treating diseases arising from sports: there is a pattern of diseases resulting from swimming, another from football, yet another from long-distance running. This does not demonstrate that these sports, or the inclination to pursue these sports, are themselves diseases. So, for instance, the fact that a doctor may be exceptionally knowledgeable about the effects of alcohol on the body, and may therefore be accepted as an expert on 'acoholism', does nothing to show that alcoholism itself is a legitimate medical concept.

Addiction, a Physical Disease?

If addiction is a disease, then presumably it's either a bodily or a mental disease. What criteria might justify defining addiction as a physical illness? Pathologists use nosology—the classification of diseases—to select, from among the phenomena they study, those that qualify as true diseases. Diseases are listed in standard pathology textbooks because they meet the nosological criteria for disease classification. A simple test of a true physical disease is whether it can be shown to exist in a corpse. There are no bodily signs of addiction itself (as opposed to its effects) that can be identified in a dead body. Addiction is therefore not listed in standard pathology textbooks.

Pathology, as revolutionized by Rudolf Virchow (1821–1902), requires an identifiable alteration in bodily tissue, a change in the cells of the body, for disease classification. No such identifiable pathology has been found in the bodies of heavy drinkers and drug users. This alone justifies the view that addiction is not a physical disease (Szasz 1991; 1994).

A symptom is subjective evidence from the patient: the patient reports certain pains and other sensations. A sign is something that can be identified in the patient's body, irrespective of the patient's reported experiences. In standard medical practice, the diagnosis of disease can be based on signs alone or on a combination of signs and symptoms, but only rarely on symptoms alone. A sign is objective physical evidence such as a lesion or chemical imbalance. Signs may be found through medical tests.

Sometimes a routine physical examination reveals signs of disease when no symptoms are reported. In such cases the disease is said to be 'asymptomatic'—without symptoms. For example, sugar in the urine combined with other signs may lead to a diagnosis of asymptomatic diabetes. Such a diagnosis is made solely on the basis of signs. It is inconceivable that addiction could ever be diagnosed on the basis of bodily signs alone. (The *effects* of heavy alcohol consumption can of course be inferred from bodily signs, but that, remember, is a different matter.) To speak of 'asymptomatic addiction' would be absurd.

True, conditions such as migraine and epilepsy are diagnosed primarily on the basis of symptoms. But, in general, it is not standard medical practice to diagnose disease on the basis of symptoms alone. The putative disease called addiction is diagnosed solely by symptoms in the form of conduct, never by signs, that is, by physical evidence in the patient's body. (A doctor might conclude that someone with cirrhosis of the liver and other bodily signs had partaken of alcoholic beverages heavily over a long period, and might infer that the patient was an 'alcoholic', but actually the doctor would be unable to distinguish this from the hypothetical case of someone who had been kept a prisoner and dosed with alcohol against her will. So, again, strictly speaking, *there cannot possibly be a bodily sign of an addiction.*)

If you visited your physician because of a dull pain in your epigastric region, would you want her to make a diagnosis without confirming it through objective tests? Wouldn't you doubt the validity of a diagnosis of heart disease without at least the results of an EKG? You would want to see reliable evidence of signs. But in the diagnosis of the disease called addiction, there are no signs, only symptoms (Szasz 1987).

We continually hear that 'addiction is a disease just like diabetes'. Yet there is no such thing as asymptomatic addiction, and *logically there could not be*. Moreover, the analogy cannot be turned around. It would be awkward to tell a person with diabetes that his condition was 'just like addiction' and inaccurate too: When a person with diabetes is deprived of insulin he will suffer and in severe cases may even die. When a heavy drinker or other drug user is deprived of alcohol or other drugs his physical health most often improves.

A Mental or Metaphorical Disease?

Mental illnesses are diagnosed on the basis of symptoms, not signs. Perhaps, then, addiction is a mental illness, a psychiatric disease. Where does it fit into the scheme of psychiatric disorders?

Psychiatric disorders can be categorized in three groups: organic disorders, functional disorders, and antisocial behavior (Szasz 1988). Organic disorders include various forms of dementia such as those caused by HIV-1 infection, acute alcohol intoxication, brain tumor or injury, dementia of the Alzheimer's type, general paresis, and multi-infarct dementia. These are physical diseases with identifiable bodily signs. Addiction has no such identifiable signs.

Functional disorders include fears (anxiety disorders), discouragements (mood disorders), and stupidities (cognitive disorders). These are mental in the sense that they involve mental activities. As Szasz has pointed out, they are diseases "only in a metaphorical sense."

Forms of antisocial behavior categorized as psychiatric illness include crime, suicide, personality disorders, and maladaptive and maladjusted behavior. Some people consider these 'disorders' because they vary from the norm and involve danger to self or others. According to Szasz, however, they are "neither 'mental' nor 'diseases'" (Szasz 1988, pp. 249–251). If addiction qualifies as an antisocial behavior, this does not necessarily imply that it is mental or a disease.

Addiction is not listed in the American Psychiatric Association's Diagnostic and Statistical Manual of Mental Disorders IV (DSM-IV). What was once listed as alcoholism is now referred to as alcohol dependence and abuse. These are listed under the category of substance-related disorders. They would not fit the category of organic disorders because they are described in terms of behavior only. They would conceivably fit the functional disorder category but probably would be subordinated to one of the established disorders such as discouragement or anxiety.

Thus, it's difficult to classify addiction as either a physical or a mental disease. Many human problems may be described *metaphorically* as diseases. We hear media pundits speak of a 'sick economy' or 'sick culture'. Declining empires, such as the Ottoman empire at the end of the nineteenth century and the Soviet empire in the 1980s, are said to be 'sick'. There is little harm in resorting to this metaphor, and therefore describing negative addictions as diseases—except that there is the danger that some people will take the metaphor literally.

Today any socially-unacceptable behavior is likely to be diagnosed as an 'addiction'. So we have shopping addiction, videogame addiction, sex addiction, Dungeons and Dragons addiction, running addiction, chocolate addiction, Internet addiction, addiction to abusive relationships, and so forth. This would be fine if it merely represented a return to the traditional, non-medical usage, in which addiction means being given over to some pursuit. However, all of these new 'addictions' are now claimed to be medical illnesses, characterized by self-destructiveness, compulsion, loss of control, and some mysterious, as-yet-unidentified physiological component. This is entirely fanciful.

People become classified as 'addicts' or 'alcoholics' because of their behavior. 'Behavior' in humans refers to intentional conduct. As was pointed out long ago by Wilhelm Dilthey, Max Weber, and

Ludwig von Mises, among others, the motions of the human body are either involuntary reflexes or meaningful human action. Human action is governed by the meaning it has for the acting person. The behavior of heavy drinking is not a form of neurological reflex but is the expression of values through action. As Herbert Fingarette puts it:

> A pattern of conduct must be distinguished from a mere sequence of reflex-like reactions. A reflex knee jerk is not conduct. If we regard something as a pattern of conduct . . . we assume that it is mediated by the mind, that it reflects consideration of reasons and preferences, the election of a preferred means to the end, and the election of the end itself from among alternatives. The complex, purposeful, and often ingenious projects with which many an addict may be occupied in his daily hustlings to maintain his drug supply are examples of conduct, not automatic reflex reactions to a singly biological cause. (1975, p. 435)

Thomas Szasz agrees that

> by behavior we mean the person's 'mode of conducting himself' or his 'deportment' . . . the name we attach to a living being's conduct in the daily pursuit of life. . . . bodily movements that are the products of neurophysiological discharges or reflexes are not behavior. . . . behavior implies action, and action implies conduct pursued by an agent seeking to attain a goal. (1987, p. 343)

The term 'alcoholism' has become so loaded with prescriptive intent that it no longer describes any drinking behavior accurately and should be abandoned. 'Heavy drinking' is a more descriptive term (Fingarette 1988). It is imprecise, but so is 'alcoholism'.

If we continue to use the term 'alcoholism', however, we should bear in mind that there is no precisely defined condition, activity, or entity called alcoholism in the way there is a precise condition known as lymphosarcoma of the mesenteric glands, for example. The actual usage of the term 'alcoholism', like 'addiction', has become primarily normative and prescriptive: a derogatory, stigmatizing word applied to people who drink 'too much'. The definition of 'too much' depends on the values of the speaker, which may be different from those of the person doing the drinking.

Calling addiction a 'disease' tells us more about the labeler than the labelee. Diseases are medical conditions. They can be discovered on the basis of bodily signs. They are something people have. They are involuntary. For example, the disease of syphilis was discovered. It is identified by specific signs. It is not a form of activity and is not based in human values. While certain behaviors increase the likelihood of acquiring syphilis, and while the acquisition of syphilis has consequences for subsequent social interaction, the behavior and the disease are separate phenomena. Syphilis meets the nosological criteria for disease classification in a pathology textbook. Unlike addiction, syphilis is a disease that can be diagnosed in a corpse.

Once we recognize that addiction cannot be classified as a literal disease, its nature as an ethical choice becomes clearer. A person starts, moderates, or abstains from drinking because that person wants to. People do the same thing with heroin, cocaine, and tobacco. Such choices reflect the person's values. The person, a moral agent, chooses to use drugs or refrains from using drugs because he or she finds meaning in doing so.

3

Do Drug Addicts
Lose It?

They are fanatics in their addictedness to the dance.
The Reader (1865)

Absolutely crucial to disease-model thinking is the theory that when addicts are taking their drug, they have 'lost control'. They supposedly cannot help themselves; they have no option but to go on taking the drug.

It's easy to see that this theory is indispensable to the disease model. Without this loss of control, how could anyone claim that the decision to take or not take some drug was not a genuine choice? 'Loss of control' has been repeatedly sought by researchers and has never been found. All the evidence we have supports the view that drug addicts are conscious—yes, even calculating —responsible persons, in full command of their behavior.

Alcoholics Control Their Drinking

Because of the legal problems involved in providing subjects with illegal substances, the most direct and conclusive investigations involve the legal drug, alcohol. Numerous studies in which alcoholics moderate or control their drinking undermine the theory alcoholics 'lose control' when drinking and utterly scotch the theory that abstinence is the only way to recovery from alcoholism. (See Bigelow et al. 1972; Cohen et al., Alcoholism, 1971; Cohen et al., Moderate Drinking, 1971; Davies 1962; Institute of Medicine 1990; Miller and Caddy 1977; Heather and Robertson 1981; Marlatt 1983; Miller 1983; Marlatt and Gordon 1985; Paredes et al. 1973; Pattison 1966; 1976; Pattison et al. 1977; Roizen, Cahalan, and Shanks 1978; Roizen 1987; Sobell, Sobell, and Christelman 1972; and Tuchfeld 1981.)

In 1962, Davies published the results of a long-term follow-up study of patients treated for alcoholism. Davies's findings were confirmed and extended by Kendell in 1965. Both studies questioned the view that abstinence is the only form of treatment for alcoholism. Seven out of the 93 recovered male alcoholics studied exhibited a pattern of normal drinking. No relationship was found between the purported physiological characteristics of alcoholics and their ability to control drinking.

The fact that some alcoholics returned to moderate drinking suggested that loss of control was a myth. An attempt was made to undermine this finding by claiming that individuals who returned to moderate drinking were not really alcoholics to begin with, but this contention could not be squared with the facts (Roizen 1987).

An important study by Merry supported Davies's findings. In Merry's 1966 study, alcoholics who were unaware they were drinking alcohol did not develop an uncontrollable desire to drink more and reported no increase in craving.

In 1971, Cohen et al. conducted a test in which five chronic alcoholics were hospitalized and given access to substantial quantities of alcohol in an effort to limit their drinking by the application of contingency management procedures. Contingency management refers to the encouragement and discouragement of behavior by rewards and punishments. These five were all 'gamma alcoholic' males, their drinking allegedly characterized by loss of control, and were admitted via the hospital emergency department in varying stages of withdrawal.

In this research, the hospitalized subjects were given the freedom to drink as much alcoholic beverage as they wished (up to 24 ounces of 95-proof ethanol on weekdays for five consecutive weeks), but were rewarded by better living conditions if they cut down on their drinking.

During the 1st, 3rd, and 5th weeks of the experiment, the contingent weeks, if the subject drank 5 ounces or less he was in the enriched environment. If he drank more than 5 ounces he was impoverished from the time he exceeded 5 ounces until 7 A.M. the next morning, plus 24 hours. He had until 7 A.M. to drink the remaining 19 ounces and during the 24-hour period following he had no access to alcohol. During the 2nd and 4th weeks, the noncontingent weeks, moderate drinking was not differentially reinforced; no matter how much the subject drank, up to 24 ounces, he was impoverished. (Cohen et al., Moderate Drinking, 1971, p. 437)

The alcoholics moderated their drinking when they were rewarded with an enriched environment. When the enriched environment was withdrawn, they returned to excessive drinking. Cohen et al. concluded they had "substantial evidence that loss of control following the first drink is not inevitable, even when the alcoholic has the opportunity to drink amounts of ethanol that approximate his customary intake outside the hospital" (p. 441). (Ethanol is the predominant form of alcohol found in alcoholic beverages. Vodka, for instance, is virtually nothing except ethanol and water.)

In 1972 and 1973 Gottheil and others tested alcoholics' ability to 'resist' the temptation of available alcohol. Many of the alcoholics studied did not drink all of the available alcohol even when given ample opportunity to do so. The findings of this study contradict the view that drinking by alcoholics necessarily results in "irresistible craving, more drinking, and loss of control." Some of the patients did not drink at all, "some drank heavily and then stopped, and some were able to drink moderately and also stop." Even among those who continued to drink heavily, "the alcohol intake varied from day to day, drinks could be resisted after large amounts had been ingested, and abstinent days alternated with drinking days."

The patients who stopped drinking "appeared to tolerate this rather well" and did not express any strong craving for alcohol. While refraining from drinking alcohol, "they slept better than they had while drinking, their self-esteem increased, they tended to experience less discomfort, and there was no significant change in withdrawal or socialization" (1973b, p. 421).

In a 1972 study, Sobell, Sobell, and Christelman concluded that the loss-of-control theory was based more on belief in the theory by alcoholics who had been taught it than on evidence that alcoholics actually did lose control. These researchers also suggested that such a belief can become a self-fulfilling prophecy.

Engle and Williams found that the desire for alcohol increased when alcoholics were told they had consumed alcohol although in fact they had not:

> The increased desire for alcohol was evidently based on the information provided or knowledge of its presence rather than on an actual physical presence and chemical effect upon the organism. No evidence was found for a physiological relation between one drink of alcohol and an increased desire for alcohol in the alcoholic. (Engle and Williams 1972, p. 1103)

Faillace et al. found no difference in the levels of craving produced by giving alcohol to alcoholics in progressively reduced amounts for up to 32 days and giving them no alcohol. The authors concluded that, at least in a controlled drinking environment,

> administering alcohol to alcoholics does not have a detrimental effect: in fact the findings suggest that such patients fare at least as well, if not better, than other alcoholics who don't receive the beverage. (1972, p. 89)

Notice that the disease-model proponents cannot say that these results are only valid for a controlled drinking environment; it's vital to their position to maintain that the environment in which drinking occurs is immaterial.

According to the loss-of-control theory, those afflicted with the disease of alcoholism cannot plan their drinking, especially when going through a period of excessive craving. In a study by leading alcoholism researchers, however, alcoholics bought and stockpiled alcohol in order to be able to get drunk in the future, even while abstaining during withdrawal from previous binges. They were able to control their drinking for psychological reasons without succumbing to an uncontrollable physiological need sparked by the use of alcohol (Mello and Mendelson 1972). The authors report that

> even in the unrestricted alcohol-access situation, no subject drank all the alcohol available or tried to 'drink to oblivion'. These data are inconsistent with predictions from the craving hypothesis so often invoked to account for an alcoholic's perpetuation of drinking. No empirical support has been provided for the notion of craving by directly observing alcoholic subjects in a situation where they can choose to drink alcohol in any volume at any time by working at a sim-

ple task. There has been no confirmation of the notion that once drinking starts, it proceeds autonomously. (pp. 159–160)

A significant experiment in 1973 supported these findings by showing that alcoholics' drinking is correlated with their beliefs about alcohol and drinking. Marlatt, Deming, and Reid successfully disguised the alcohol content of beverages given to a randomly assigned group of sixty-four alcoholic and social drinkers (the latter were the control group) asked to participate in a "taste-rating task." One group of subjects was given a beverage with alcohol and was told that, although it tasted like alcohol it contained none. The other group was given a "tonic" beverage with no alcohol and told it did contain alcohol. Among both the alcoholics and the social drinkers, "the consumption rates were higher in those conditions in which subjects were led to believe they would consume alcohol, regardless of the actual beverage administered" (1973, p. 240).

People who have taken the drug Antabuse quickly experience acute physical distress if they then consume even a tiny amount of alcohol. There's no doubt that people on Antabuse will not consume alcohol—if they try it once they will never repeat it, but usually, knowing what to expect, they don't try it even once. Is Antabuse then useful for 'treating' heavy drinking? Quite useless. The drinker simply stops taking Antabuse, *waits several days for the drug to clear out of his system*, and then drinks alcohol. What does this tell us?

Further support for a psychological explanation can be found in studies on spontaneous remission among alcoholics. ('Spontaneous remission' means that symptoms go away 'by themselves'. In this context, it means that formerly heavy drinkers stop drinking or moderate, without outside help.) These studies have found that some alcoholics choose to give up drinking on the basis of significant life events (Tuchfeld 1981; Roizen, Cahalan, and Shanks 1978).

Is Marijuana a Gateway Drug?

Most people who have used marijuana 'mature out' of it. This means that they use it for a while and then either moderate their use or give it up altogether, for any number of reasons. We have come a long way from the days of *Reefer Madness,* and nearly everyone understands today that marijuana does not produce a physiological compulsion to continue consuming it. A very high proportion of the population have tried marijuana at some time, yet very few are actually in the habit of using it frequently at any given time.

Many people no longer think of marijuana as either 'psychologically' or 'physiologically' addicting. It's recognized that marijuana users neither feel compelled to use marijuana as a way of coping with the world nor feel compelled to use it because withdrawal from use would create intolerable physical symptoms. These discredited views have been replaced by the claim that consumption of marijuana leads on to 'harder' drugs like cocaine and heroin.

Contrary to claims that marijuana is a 'gateway' drug, the scientific research shows that most people who use marijuana either tried it and stopped, use only marijuana and do not move on to those supposedly harder drugs, or used it occasionally and then stopped for diverse psychological and social reasons.

It's indeed true that many people who use heroin, cocaine, and other 'hard' drugs may have 'started with' marijuana. But that doesn't mean that their use of marijuana caused them to use those other drugs. Most people who consume whiskey have earlier consumed coffee, most people who consume coffee have earlier consumed water, and most people who consume water have earlier consumed human breast milk or infant formula, but this does not show that breast milk or formula causes consumption of whiskey.

No correlation has been properly established between marijuana use and later heroin use, for example. But even if such a correlation were shown, we would be a long way from concluding that marijuana consumption was a cause of later heroin consumption. For example, it could be that the reasons for heroin use are similar to the reasons for marijuana use. In other words, it might not be that there is something in marijuana that causes a move to heroin, but rather that consumers are looking for the same thing in heroin they derived from marijuana. The causal relation runs from the person's psychology to both marijuana and heroin. If heroin had been cheaper and more easily available than marijuana, the person might just as easily have moved in the other direction, from heroin to marijuana.

Marijuana Smokers Control Their Smoking

An excellent book on the facts about marijuana is *Marijuana Myths, Marijuana Facts* (Zimmer and Morgan 1997). However, there are still some shortcomings in their presentation. There is a disease-model connotation in their use of the word 'dependence', and occasionally a cursory interpretation and generalization of marijuana research that may encourage inaccurate inferences.

I think one should be cautious, as well as responsible, about drug-taking. Zimmer and Morgan do not even mention possibilities of harmful effects which have admittedly not been demonstrated but which we are a long way from ruling out. While this has nothing to do with involuntariness, I have come to suspect through long experience in counseling marijuana users that heavy marijuana consumption may adversely affect people's ability to differentiate between what they know and what they imagine. I also suspect that those effects will vary from person to person based on levels of their self-esteem and self-efficacy, as well as the extent to which individuals grew up in environments which encouraged them to feel guilty about themselves, the extent to which they were encouraged to view themselves and the world in dichotomous or 'absolutist' ways, and whether or not they had trouble forming a clear sense of identity during adolescence.

Zimmer and Morgan do accurately review important research that bears on our understanding of marijuana and addiction. The conclusions are at odds with the propaganda of past 'wars on drugs', and in line with our commonsense impressions:

> Epidemiological surveys indicate that the large majority of people who try marijuana do not become long-term frequent users. A study of adults in their thirties, who were first surveyed in high school, found a high 'discontinuation rate' for marijuana. Of those who had tried marijuana, 75 percent had not used it in the past year and 85 percent had not used it in the past month. . . . Eleven percent had used it in the past year and 2.5 percent had used it an average of once a week or more. Only 0.8 percent of Americans currently smoke marijuana on a daily or near-daily basis. (Zimmer and Morgan 1997, p. 27)

Cocaine Users Control Their Cocaine Consumption

Similar findings have been reported in studies of alleged cocaine, including crack, 'dependence'. Patricia G. Erickson and her colleagues at the former Addiction Research Foundation in Ontario (now the Center for Addiction and Mental Health), after reviewing many studies on cocaine, concluded, in their book *The Steel Drug*, that "most social-recreational users are able to maintain a low-to-moderate use pattern without escalating to dependency and that users can essentially 'treat themselves'" (Erickson et al. 1987, p. 54). Many users "particularly appreciated that they could benefit from the various appealing effects of cocaine without a feeling of loss of control" (p. 81).

"The drug literature often singles out cocaine as a powerfully addictive drug . . . and points with alarm to the growing number of treatment admissions for cocaine dependence . . . The prevalent 'disease model' of cocaine addiction usually asserts that exposure to cocaine causes addiction, that claims of moderate cocaine use entail 'denial' of addiction by the user, and that apparently nonaddicted users will eventually become addicted" (Erickson and Alexander 1989; in Schaler 1998a, p. 271).

Erickson and Alexander review the available evidence on cocaine's 'addictive liability', the likelihood that use will lead to 'addiction' (defined as someone giving a much higher priority to drug use than to other behaviors that previously had higher values). They conclude that cocaine's addictive liability "does not appear to be extraordinarily high." It's estimated that of those who try cocaine, around 5–10 percent progress to "more frequent use." Of these, 10–25 percent progress to "compulsive use" (p. 285). So at most 2.5 percent of those who try cocaine will become 'addicts' in the conventional sense, and (though Erickson and Alexander do not make this point here) most of those will mature out of their addiction with the passage of time.

Erickson and co-authors (1987) cite a study by Spotts and Shontz (1980) that provided "the most in-depth profile of intravenous cocaine users to date." They state: "most users felt a powerful attachment to cocaine, but not to the extent of absolute necessity. . . . all agreed that cocaine is not physically addicting . . . many reported temporary tolerance." In a study by Siegel (1984) of

118 users, 99 of whom were social-recreational users, described by Erickson et al. as the only longitudinal study of cocaine users in North America, "all users reported episodes of cocaine abstinence."

> [Research findings] call into question many of the prevailing assumptions about cocaine's inevitably destructive power over lives, careers, and health, and provide empirical evidence about a different reality. (Erickson and Weber 1994; in Schaler 1998a, p. 291)

Cocaine users moderate their use of the drug for psychological and social reasons that are important to them. Those reasons vary from person to person. Since cocaine consumers moderate their use, they are evidently not enslaved, either psychologically or physically, by cocaine addiction. If they were enslaved and out of control, they would presumably maintain their use of the drug rigorously, or steadily escalate it, or consume as much as was available.

Some people do cause their own death through their immoderate use of cocaine, but this is not common. Research shows that "compulsive, destructive use is rare"; that escalation in the use of cocaine is only one pattern and "often the reverse occurs"; that "moderate use" of cocaine "without harmful effects is possible"; that controlled use of cocaine is "the norm"; that "little or no harm results to most users"; and that "most users are law-abiding, apart from their drug-related behavior" (Erickson and Weber 1994).

The findings of studies on cocaine use among high school students are consistent with those I've just mentioned:

> Most of those who used [cocaine] in high school do not show a cross-time progression to heavier use in the three to four years following graduation, which suggests that dependence either develops rather slowly or develops with relatively low frequency among moderate and light users. (Johnston, O'Malley, and Bachman 1986, p. 221)

According to recent investigation, crack cocaine is no more 'addictive' and no less a matter of personal volition than the more traditional cocaine (Erickson et al. 1994; Reinarman and Levine 1997).

We should evaluate the claims of cocaine users objectively: Disease-model proponents often say that cocaine users who say they can and do moderate their consumption are 'in denial'. But given that the scientific evidence corroborates that claim, we would do better to view with suspicion those cocaine users who claim they *cannot* stop using the drugs. There simply is no evidence to support that claim, though 'addicts' soon learn that it is what therapists, social workers, and 'treatment' providers want to hear.

There is a saying in AA about 'alcoholics' (drunks): 'The first thing to go is the truth'. There is also a saying in law enforcement circles that 'all addicts are liars'. These doubts as to the veracity of the 'alcoholic' or 'addict' are not usually applied to their claims of powerlessness. The evidence demonstrates that people do moderate their use of cocaine at will. Even those claiming uncontrollable cravings themselves go in and out of use. If the drug is withheld or unavailable, they don't die or run screaming through the streets. They simply long for their drug, in exactly the same way that we all long for any number of pleasures, activities, and experiences, if deprived of them. Cocaine users are fundamentally no different from other people: they are struggling with the experience of being human.

Heroin Addicts Control Their Use of Heroin

All the above findings tend to support the broad view that drug use is a 'function' of psychological, not physiological, 'variables'. (Sorry for the jargon, but ordinary language does not lend itself to talking about such relationships without implying causation.) Heroin, long considered the hardest drug, is no different. A notable study of 943 randomly selected Vietnam veterans, 495 of whose urine samples tested positive for opiates when they came back from from Vietnam, was commissioned by the U.S. Department of Defense and led by epidemiologist Lee N. Robins. This study shows that only 14 percent of those who used heroin in Vietnam returned to heroin use after returning to the United States. Robins's findings support the theory that drug use is a function of environmental stress, which in this example ceased when the veterans left Vietnam.

Veterans said they used heroin to cope with the harrowing experience of war. I think the soldiers in Vietnam used heroin to *avoid* coping with environmental stress. I do mean to use the word 'avoid' here, despite criticism from my colleagues for doing so. The fact of the matter is that, whether avoiding coping with environmental stress is a good thing or a bad thing, the soldiers who used heroin in Vietnam chose to use heroin rather than deal with their stress in 'constructive' ways. These constructive ways include changing their environment somehow, which, granted, may have been very difficult to do. Or they may have included changing the way they perceived their environment, which again may have been very difficult. By changing the way they perceive their environment I do not mean retreating, psychologically, to pretending that what was occurring in their environment was not really occurring, or pretending that what they were feeling was not what they were really feeling. After all, most soldiers in Vietnam *didn't* use heroin. Why not? As Robins and her co-authors wrote in *Archives of General Psychiatry*,

> it does seem clear that the opiates are not so addictive that use is necessarily followed by addiction nor that once addicted, an individual is necessarily addicted permanently. At least in certain circumstances, individuals can use narcotics regularly and even become addicted to them but yet be able to avoid use in other social circumstances. . . . How generalizable these results are is currently unknown. No previous study has had so large and so unbiased a sample of heroin users. (Robins, Helzer, and Davis 1975, pp. 961)

The cocaine and heroin studies I've mentioned challenge the contention that drug addiction is primarily characterized by loss of control. These studies and a number of others, support the idea that what goes on outside of a person's body is more significant in understanding drug use, including alcoholism, than what goes on inside the body.

The study by Robins and her colleagues was tremendously important for public discussion of addiction. Their findings ran counter to everything that used to make up the conventional wisdom on heroin and addiction, and have only slowly been seeping through into broader public awareness. Journalists and politicians, of course, are always the last to hear about anything of importance.

Does use of heroin rapidly progress to frequent or regular use? Robins et al. found no significant difference for heroin when compared to amphetamines and marijuana in terms of progression to daily or regular use, for those veterans who purchased heroin on the streets of the United States in 1974.

Is heroin use so much more pleasurable than the use of other drugs that it supplants them? They found the exact opposite, to wit:

veterans who used heroin in the last two years were more likely to use every common drug during that same period than were veterans who did not use heroin. . . the typical pattern of the heroin user seems to be to use a wide variety of drugs plus alcohol. The stereotype of the heroin addict as someone with a monomaniacal craving for a single drug seems hardly to exist in this sample. Heroin addicts use many other drugs, and not only casually or in desperation. (Robins et al. 1980; reprinted in Schaler 1998a, pp. 254–55)

Is heroin addiction more or less permanent unless there is prolonged treatment? They found "no better results for treated than untreated men whether treated in Vietnam or later" and "that treatment is certainly not always necessary for remission . . . craving can occur and can be extremely persistent . . . but it seems that prolonged craving is a rare residual effect of heroin addiction" (pp. 256–57).

Does maintaining recovery from heroin addiction require abstention from heroin? Absolutely not. Heroin users can and do go in and out of using heroin.

Perhaps an even more surprising finding than the high proportion of men who recovered from addiction after Vietnam was the number who went back to heroin without becoming readdicted . . . half of the men who had been addicted in Vietnam used heroin on their return but only one-eighth became readdicted to heroin. Even when heroin was used frequently, that is, more than once a week for a considerable period of time, only one-half of those who used it frequently became readdicted. (pp. 258–59)

And finally, they asked, is heroin use itself a major social problem? And once again their findings were the opposite of conventional thinking on the subject:

Our findings are that the *occasional* use of . . .[heroin, amphetamines, and barbiturates] was not associated with a significant increase in social adjustment problems. *Regular* use of each of these drugs except marijuana, again defined as use more than once a week for more than a month, was associated with an increase in social adjustment problems. . . .the association of heroin with social problems was less statistically significant than was the effect of either amphetamines or barbiturates.

Thus the reason that we find higher levels of social disability among heroin users than among users of other drugs is probably attributable to the kinds of people who use heroin. Men disposed to social problems are likely to use drugs, and those with the very greatest predisposition to social problems are the ones likely to use heroin. (Robins et al. 1980; reprinted in Schaler 1998a, p. 264).

What We Can Learn from Rat Park

The studies I've discussed in this chapter tell strongly against the claim that addiction, be it to alcohol, marijuana, cocaine, or heroin, is involuntary. Addiction, regardless of drug, is a choice. That alcohol, marijuana, cocaine, and heroin users all moderate or control their use of the drug at one time or another, if not regularly, tends to undermine the idea that addiction is involuntary.

It might occur to some people to respond to the studies I've reviewed above by saying that the subjects were obviously 'not really addicted'. This opens up intriguing lines of enquiry, like how we could tell that these subjects weren't really addicted and how we would ever go about finding the elusive 'really addicted' people. Furthermore, anyone rejecting the findings of addiction research on that basis would have to accept that large numbers of people can regularly consume alcohol, marijuana, heroin, or cocaine without becoming 'addicted' to these substances. That would be almost as serious a jolt to conventional thinking as acknowledging that addiction is a choice.

The reader may suspect that I am being one-sided in giving only the research which goes against the loss of control theory. But there simply is no empirical research corroborating the existence of 'loss of control' in alcoholics or any other addicts. The only research sometimes cited in support is research on laboratory animals. Some early studies were done in which monkeys or rats were able to press a lever to give themselves doses of cocaine. They tended to dose themselves heavily, sometimes even in preference to food, lose weight rapidly, experience convusions, and die. Reports of such experiments were gleefully repeated in the popular culture as showing what would necessarily happen to any mammal given free access to cocaine or to an opiate.

Now, if that were all there was to it, we could make a number of skeptical observations, most notably: 1. that this behavior by lab monkeys and rats completely contradicts the observed behavior of human drug consumers; and 2. that humans have more capacity to think about remote consequences of their actions, and to make their behavior comply with cultural rules, than other mammals.

More recent research, however, has shown these early studies in a completely new light. Monkeys and rats, like humans, are naturally sociable and exploratory animals. To keep them under standard lab conditions, in solitary confinement in a small cage, unable even to see another member of their species, is unrelenting torture. In this situation, the hapless animal subjects were given a lever to press—virtually the only thing they could do except sit there passively.

Psychologist Bruce Alexander and his colleagues at Simon Fraser University in British Columbia were interested in seeing what would happen with animals in a freer, less stressful environment. Alexander theorized that animals, human and non-human alike, consume drugs as a way of coping with their environmental experience, not because they become enslaved due to any physiological change or chemical property of the drug. They conducted a unique long-term experiment called 'Rat Park'. The results of the first four years of observing rats in Rat Park were published in the *British Columbia Medical Journal* in 1980.

Alexander's team placed rats in two environments. One was 'normal housing' for lab animals, individual cages mounted on steel racks, constructed so that the animals could not see or touch each other.

> The second environment was the most natural habitat we could contrive in the laboratory, so we named it 'Rat Park'. Rat Park is open and spacious, with about 200 times the square footage of the standard cage. It is also scenic (with a peaceful British Columbia forest painted on the plywood walls), comfortable (with empty tin cans and other desiderata strewn about the floor), and friendly (we ran co-ed groups of sixteen to twenty rats). (Alexander, Hadaway, and Coambs 1980; reprinted in Schaler 1998a, p. 267)

Two drinkable liquids were provided for rats in both environments. One was sugary, laced with morphine. (Practically speaking, morphine is the same as heroin and the effects of swallowing it are the same as those of injecting it.) The other had no morphine. The taste of both solutions was similar.

The first results were a big surprise. Rats in both environments drank the harmless solution almost exclusively, avoiding the morphine solution. The researchers then made the morphine solution progressively sweeter in both environments (rats have a very sweet tooth), while leaving the non-morphine solution the same, in an attempt to 'seduce' the rats into consuming morphine. In other phases of the experiment, Alexander's team gave the rats no choice but to drink the morphine for 57 days (compelling them to become completely habituated to it), then allowed them a choice once again:

> No matter how much we induced, seduced, or tempted them, the Rat Park rats resisted drinking the narcotic solution. The caged rats drank plenty, however, ranging up to *sixteen times* as much as the Rat Park residents in one experimental phase, and measuring ten times as much in some other phases. The females, curiously, drank more morphine in both environments, but the Rat Park rats always drank far less than the caged rats.

The Rat Park study provides very strong support for the idea that 'environment' and 'coping' are much better predictors of opiate consumption than availability of the drug, chemical properties of the drug, or any conjectured 'physiological addiction' characterized by tolerance or withdrawal. An outcome similar to that of Rat Park was found in a study of rats, some housed in isolation and some in groups, injecting themselves with cocaine (Schenk et al. 1987).

It may well be that there is something naturally pleasurable to mammals about consuming opiates, but the anesthetic and tranquilizing effects, themselves responsible for that pleasure, also reduce the pleasure derived from other activities such as playing, eating, sex, or social interaction. Rats are apparently able to act upon that trade-off, but are less inclined to do so if those other sources of pleasure are shut down.

Solitary confinement in a narrow space is harrowing for a rat or for a human. If we want to understand why some people become heavy consumers of drugs, we should ask what it is in their lives that constitutes for them the emotional equivalent of being 'in solitary'.

Risky, Unwise, or Self-Destructive Choices

Many people will point to the fact that drug consumers sometimes die from the consequences of their drug use, and conclude that anyone who self-destructs through the use of a drug, such as cocaine, must be doing so involuntarily.

Such a conclusion would be hasty. People engage in all kinds of risky behavior which may sometimes lead to their deaths: skiing,

sky diving, marathon running, mountain climbing, stock car rac-
ing, and horseback riding all entail high risks of personal injury.
Other people ruin themselves financially by taking risks, either in
gambling or trading in financial markets. Having ruined themselves financially, they sometimes kill themselves. Others run high
health risks through promiscuous, unprotected sex. Yet others get
into fights, either on their own account or that of the rulers of their
country, or set themselves up as martyrs by joining some despised
religious movement.

There are some disease-model imperialists who would no doubt
gladly accept the conclusion that all of the above are diseases—all
foolish or ill-advised choices are not really choices but symptoms!
But most of us will recoil from such a preposterous conclusion. We
will acknowledge that it is indeed possible to make a genuine
choice, or a succession of such choices, that is very bad. A bad
choice remains a choice.

If any reader is still hesitant to agree that addiction is not a disease but a choice, I would like to offer that reader a mental exercise. Is it *ever possible* for people to make genuine choices, not the
symptoms of a disease, which are unwise, excessively risky, or self-
destructive? If your answer is *no*, then just contemplate the vast
extent of human affairs which you are allocating to the sphere of
medicine. *Any* way in which folk contrive to screw up their lives
becomes an illness. If your answer is yes, then please explain how
we can distinguish those genuine choices, not symptoms of a disease, from involuntary compulsions, symptoms of a disease.

A further thought: if the very bad things people do are always
involuntary, not chosen, what about the good things they do?
Shouldn't we consider Mother Teresa, Bill Gates, or Albert Einstein
victims of a disease which compelled them to help the destitute,
improve the world's software, or dream up better physical theories?
Since they had no choice, they can surely deserve no credit. If not,
why not?

4

How Beliefs Affect Reality

This bird is addicted to hot countries.

Surflet and Markham (1616)

In olden times many people believed in demon possession or in witches' spells. They used these imaginary entities to explain their behavior, but their belief in these entities also in fact influenced their behavior. The beliefs people hold today about addiction influence their thoughts and actions, both as addicts and as addiction treatment providers. Whereas the theories we hold about the structure of the atom or the evolution of life do not affect the way the world works, popular theories of addiction do greatly influence how addicts think and behave.

The Self-Fulfilling Prophecy

The more people believe in their ability to moderate their consumption of drugs and alcohol, the more likely they will be to moderate. The converse is also true: the more people believe in their inability to moderate their consumption of drugs and alcohol, the more likely they will be not to moderate.

Most treatment programs teach people to believe they lack the ability to moderate their consumption of drugs. The more treatment programs convince clients this is true, the more likely the clients are to prove them 'correct'. That's because consuming drugs irresponsibly (like consuming drugs moderately) involves the intention to do so. There is no force alien to oneself that is responsible for one's behavior.

The beliefs of 'addiction-treatment providers' are important as well. What they believe about drugs, addiction, disease, authority, and personal and 'higher' powers largely dictates their behavior toward clients. Knowing more about the beliefs treatment providers hold dear can thus help us to comprehend what is done in the name of treatment for addiction (see Chapter 7 below). Regardless of whether treatment providers' beliefs about addiction are true or false, rational or irrational, those beliefs largely shape their actions.

Something similar has happened in our attempts to help drug users (those who want help) in what's called addiction 'treatment'. Because what occurs in the name of treatment is based on certain beliefs people assert as truth about addiction, treatment is a disaster—it's a problem masquerading as a solution. In other words, our inaccurate and essentially religious-based beliefs about addiction become self-fulfilling prophecies (Schaler 1996b).

Teaching people in 'treatment' for addiction problems that they 'don't know they have a problem' may create a problem for them. Teaching them that they cannot control themselves may convince them that they cannot control themselves. Teaching them to believe that 'treatment' is the only solution to their problem may persuade them that they cannot solve problems on their own. It reinforces dependency. Teaching them that addiction is all-or-nothing may influence them to believe they can never be anything other than sick. Teaching them they're powerless encourages them to act powerless. Teaching them that abstinence is the only way to control their addiction may make them think that whenever they are not totally abstinent, they are out of control. Then, when they do take the drug, they make themselves feel as if they are out of control. The middle ground of St. Paul's 'moderation in all things' is denied to them.

Teaching 'addicts' that they are physically different from 'normal' people tacitly gives them permission to act irresponsibly when they consume too much of their drug, as does teaching them that addiction is a hereditary defect. Teaching them that they can never mature out of their addiction and are always in danger of relapsing tends to make them feel hopeless and helpless. There is nothing they can do about it! All they can ever do to change their behavior is abstain and pray.

Drug War Propaganda

The metaphor of a 'war on drugs' is aptly chosen. Truth is the first casualty. The more we keep losing, the more we hear that victory is in sight. And, just as, in an international war, the enemy is demonized by atrocity stories, which sometimes have a basis in fact but are always embellished and exaggerated, so in the War on Drugs, inaccurate 'atrocity' stories about the effects of drugs are disseminated.

Just as it becomes a form of disloyalty to question the government's atrocity stories about a foreign enemy, so it becomes dangerous and 'irresponsible' to question the government's exaggerated scare stories about drugs. The thinking seems to be that drugs are so terrible that it can only do good to misrepresent them as being even worse than they are.

Our children are deluged with false information about drugs and addiction. They are the targets of scare tactics by anti-drug fundamentalists. Many children discount anything adults tell them about the dangers of drug use, because the children know that much of what they're taught is false. They see their friends and others using drugs with consequences different from the ones they're taught to expect.

Just consider the publicity given to the public exposure and disciplining of athletes who have taken drugs like cocaine. Amid all the sanctimonious hypocrisy and cant, what is the one certain thing that any intelligent child will infer from these drug scandals? The fact that one can take drugs and be a terrific athlete! The effects of anti-drug propaganda are dangerous. By teaching, often coercively, falsehoods about drugs—for example, that drugs are universally-addicting substances and that drug users are sick—anti-drug propagandists succeed in teaching children something completely different from what they intended to teach them.

What the kids learn is the false and dangerous notion that people cannot hurt themselves with drugs. Moreover, anti-drug zealots fail to understand that children learn more from the way adults think and behave than from what adults preach.

Learning from the Navajo

The belief that one is powerless and that one's actions are somehow controlled by forces other than one's own choices is discouraging and demoralizing. I believe we should promote beliefs favorable to self-efficacy. I also believe we can learn from traditional Navajo concepts.

The commonsense concept of self-efficacy is highly consistent with the Navajo concept of *hozho*. This is the most important concept in traditional Navajo culture; it "combines the concepts of beauty, goodness, order, harmony, and everything that is positive or ideal" (Carrese and Rhodes 1995). For example, Navajo say

> 'Think and speak in a positive way.' This theme is encompassed by the Navajo phrases *hoshooji nitsihakees* and *hoshooji saad*. The literal translations are 'think in the Beauty Way' and 'talk in the Beauty Way.' The prominence of these themes reflects the Navajo view that thought and language have the power to shape reality and control events . . . [They reflect] the Navajo view that health is maintained and restored through positive ritual language. (Carrese and Rhodes 1995)

Navajo consciously avoid thinking or speaking in a negative way, using the phrase *Doo djiniidah* ('Don't talk that way!'). I think we should apply this to the nine tenets of the disease-model credo. These beliefs are not only unfounded, they are destructive, and we shouldn't 'talk that way'.

As people come to believe they can develop other ways to deal with life instead of relying on drugs or alcohol, they gain confidence in their ability to determine their own destiny. As they come to believe that addiction has more to do with the environments they live in than with the drugs they use (a clear indication of research), they may further realize they have the power to change those environments to help themselves. They may recognize *they* are the 'higher power'. To disease modelists, that is sacrilege.

When people understand how many people outgrow drug and alcohol addiction, they realize their own addiction problems are solvable. When heavy drinkers and drug users learn they have the ability to moderate their drinking or drug use, they are naturally more likely to fulfill that belief in their ability. When they recognize drug and alcohol addiction is a behavior they choose to engage in when life is going badly, they're more likely to do something to improve their life. When people believe they can rely on themselves to overcome an addiction, they're more likely to mobilize the necessary inner strength to change their behavior. When drug addicts and alcoholics believe they can find their own ways out of addiction, without outside help, given the opportunity, they're more likely to emerge from despair and build a life they value more than a life of drugs alone. Most importantly when people believe drug addiction is mainly a way of life, a behavior people engage in as a way to avoid coping with the world—and not something they're hopelessly imprisoned in—they may be more inclined to make the necessary changes not only in their own world but in the world they live in. People can learn what's necessary to live a meaningful life and put that knowledge to positive effect.

Each of these beliefs results in a more positive and common-sense outlook consistent with scientific principles established through self-efficacy research, and consistent with the Navajo concept of *hozho*. We all create self-fulfilling prophecies for ourselves based on our beliefs. What people believe to be true about themselves dictates how they behave in the world.

The Menace of the Disease Model

A few months ago the parents of a 16-year-old girl brought her to me for help with her drug problem. I will call this girl 'Zoey'. A county social worker had referred the parents to me. No one had been able to help them. They handed me the social worker's prognosis on Zoey and it looked grim.

In our first session, Zoey's mother apologized to her for telling her she was possessed by the Devil. She had been using LSD and marijuana regularly. The mother took Zoey out of the public high school she'd been attending because of her concern that Zoey was being badly influenced by her friends there. Zoey's mother was undoubtedly right about that.

After our family session I spoke with Zoey alone for 30 minutes. She was definitely showing many of the effects of chronic drug use. At the end of the session, Zoey said I was different from the many other 'shrinks' she'd seen.

I asked her what she'd learned about addiction from all the different treatment experiences she'd had. She replied that addiction was a disease, and then rattled off all the canned myths of the disease model. I told her the idea that addiction was a disease was completely wrong, that taking drugs was her choice, and that she had the power to control herself whenever she wanted to. I told her all the therapists who'd told her differently were full of sheer nonsense. She was visibly shocked, but finally said she agreed with me.

I worked with Zoey over the next few months, and as usual, I kept the emphasis off drugs and asked her about the problems in her life. I will now omit many important developments, and simply say that for several months Zoey has been completely abstinent from drugs, except for a few very moderate intakes of alcoholic beverage. She still associates with people who smoke marijuana, but she doesn't smoke it with them.

At first, Zoey's mother couldn't believe it, despite the improvement in her behavior, but she had her urine tested and it came back clean. Zoey's mother told me how she wept when she saw the report and knew that Zoey really was off drugs.

Now we get to the interesting part. Zoey wanted to go to a special school that is part of the public school system. It's a special school for kids who have had trouble with drugs. She didn't want to go there because she needed the school's help, but because she didn't want the hassle of going back to her regular public school, where there was intense peer pressure to take drugs. She applied for admission to the special school and was interviewed by the principal.

The principal asked her about her drug problem and called it a disease. Zoey replied that she'd learned it wasn't a disease but a choice. She told the principal she had the power to control her behavior, and had not taken drugs for several months.

The principal denied her admission to the school. Remember, this is a public school, and Zoey is being denied admission solely on account of her beliefs, specifically her belief that addiction is a choice. The principal told Zoey that she had the wrong attitude and that she would never get better with that attitude. She encouraged

Zoey to get 'treatment' for her problem and to go to Twelve-Step meetings. In the principal's mind, Zoey was sick because she refused to accept that she had the disease of addiction and that she could not make a voluntary choice. The fact that Zoey is not taking drugs is not considered material.

What mattered to the principal was what Zoey believed. That Zoey believed something contradicting the disease model proved that Zoey was sick with drug addiction. The treatment is to change her opinions, to accept that addiction is involuntary and that she cannot control herself.

Zoey is now back at her regular public school with its powerful social pressure to take drugs, but so far she has resisted temptation.

Don't think that this is a bizarre, isolated incident. This kind of thing happens all the time. Several years ago two college students of mine were arrested for bringing marijuana into the U.S. from Jamaica. Although they smoked pot occasionally, their main motive in bringing it in was to make money.

After a month in jail and numerous hearings, they were ordered into treatment. I met with one of these students a few years later, as he was a straight-A student who now wanted my assistance in getting him into law school, which I was more than happy to give. We went over the whole sorry story.

The two had been ordered into multiple and weekly meetings for therapy and Twelve-Step groups for many months. At one point one of the students told a therapist that he'd brought the drugs into the country to make money which he needed for school and other expenses, and that having to attend all these therapy and Twelve-Step sessions was getting in the way of his school studies.

The therapist replied that it didn't matter whether he failed college. The important thing was that he was being treated for his disease. Any disagreement with the therapist or with the Twelve-Step religion was labeled 'denial', a symptom of the disease. Eventually, this student went along with the nonsense, was pronounced cured, finished college, and was released from treatment.

This is the reality of 'treatment' in the U.S. today. It's like something out of Kafka. With the current move to 'decriminalize' by 'medicalizing', I can foresee the day when all those who take drugs will be provided with those drugs at taxpayers' expense, and pronounced 'cured' because they announce that they have no choice, whereas those who do not take drugs will be incarcerated in treatment centers because they have the disease of addiction, as demonstrated by the symptom that they claim to have a choice.

Addiction Treatments Don't Work

A favorite device of addiction treatment practitioners and of many present-day therapists is to accuse their patients of 'denial'. Denial means refusal to accept the therapist's opinion of yourself and your problems. Denial is itself always a symptom of the disease diagnosed by the therapist. Hence, your rejection of your therapist's diagnosis proves that diagnosis correct. (Along parallel lines, try this: 'I suspected my patient might have diabetes, but when he rejected that idea, I knew for certain that he had diabetes. Denial is one of the typical stratagems of a confirmed diabetic.')

Typically, addiction treatment providers insist that their patients acknowledge they are addicts or alcoholics, and powerless to do anything about it. If a drug consumer protests that he takes drugs because he enjoys it, the therapist will conclude that this demonstrates the patient's involuntary addiction.

Now, while treatment providers routinely diagnose drug users as being 'in denial', the treatment providers themselves deny the fact that treatment generally doesn't work. I'll repeat that: *addiction treatments do not work*. This doesn't mean that individuals never give up their addiction after treatment. It's simply that they don't seem to do so at any higher rate than without treatment. One treatment tends to be just about as effective as any other treatment, which is just about as effective as no treatment at all. The situation has been accurately summed up by Edwards et al.:

> It is not only that the research literature is poor in reports which suggest that any particular treatment is advantageous; on the contrary it is rich in reports which demonstrate that a given treatment is no better than another. (Edwards et al. 1977, p. 1026)

We hear a continual clamor for 'more addiction treatment'. The public is rarely told just how utterly ineffective all treatment programs actually are. Treatment professionals know this all too well. The best predictor of treatment success, says Charles Schuster, former director of the National Institute on Drug Abuse, is whether the addict has a job or not.

You sometimes hear, usually from those who want to decriminalize drugs by medicalizing addiction, of very impressive treatment successes in Europe. These are cases where the government maintains the addicts in their drug habit, in some cases with the identical drug (such as heroin), in other cases with a close substitute (methadone instead of heroin). The government supplies the addict with the drug for the rest of the addict's life—that's counted as a 'success'.

George Vaillant, now professor of psychiatry at Harvard Medical School, describes his first experience, using the disease model and its effectiveness in diagnosing alcoholism, in *The Natural History of Alcoholism* (1983):

> I learned for the first time how to diagnose alcoholism as an illness
> . . . Instead of pondering the sociological and psychodynamic complexities of alcoholism, . . . alcoholism became a fascinating disease
> . . . by inexorably moving patients into the treatment system of AA, I
> was working for the most exciting alcohol program in the world. . .
> After initial discharge, only five patients in the Clinic sample never
> relapsed to alcoholic drinking, and there is compelling evidence that
> the results of our treatment were no better than the natural history of
> the disease. (pp. 283–84)

The Disease Model's Catch–22

In a careful review of studies on treatment success and follow-up studies of heroin addicts at the United States Public Health Service hospital for narcotics addicts at Lexington, Kentucky, where "tens of thousands of addicts have been treated," the late Edward M. Brecher concluded in *Licit and Illicit Drugs*: "Almost all [addicts] became readdicted and reimprisoned . . . for most the process is repeated over and over again . . . [and] no cure for narcotics addiction, and no effective deterrent, was found there—or anywhere else" (1972, p. 71). Brecher reviewed research by, among others, Vaillant. Brecher agreed that the reasearch supported the disease theory.

Brecher explained the failure of treatment in terms of the alleged addictive property of heroin. Vaillant suggested that tuberculosis be considered an analogy. Treatment, he said, rests entirely on recognition of the factors contributing to the "resistance" of the patient. And here is the 'Catch–22' of the disease modelists: addiction is a disease beyond volitional control except when it comes to treatment failure, where the addict's stubborn 'resistance' comes into play.

Vaillant performed a twelve-year follow-up study of New York City addicts admitted to the USPHS Hospital at Lexington, Kentucky. He convincingly showed that treatment was ineffective: "Virtually all patients who had been physically addicted and did not die relapsed. After leaving, 79 percent of the discharged patients used several shots of narcotics a day for at least 12 months" (1965, p. 730). This high rate of "relapse" following treatment confirmed Vaillant's belief in the disease theory.

Vaillant also observed that with the passing of the years, many of the addicts abandoned drug-taking. When last contacted in the twelve-year follow-up, 46 percent were "off drugs and in the community. Thirty percent had been abstinent for the last 3 to 12 years" (p. 736). Vaillant concluded that "the concept that addicts 'burn out' or 'mature out' of addiction must be entertained," and mentioned Winnick's conjecture that "in their thirties, perhaps two-thirds of all addicts become spontaneously abstinent" (Vaillant 1965, p. 734).

Vaillant's findings seem to be consistent with the following picture, which I believe is roughly accurate. Of those labeled both 'addicts' and 'anti-social criminals', a small number, maybe 10 percent, abandon drugs within a short space of time, with or without treatment, and a much larger number, the majority, mature out of heavy drug use over a period of years, with or without treatment.

Ironically, the fact that addiction treatment does not work helps to convince people in the addiction treatment field that addiction is a disease. What else could account for the tenacity with which addicts cling to their addictions? Could it be that people sometimes freely choose to do foolish and self-destructive things? Inconceivable! It must be a disease that makes them do it.

Notice the subtle reasoning of the addiction treatment industry. It's an open secret that addiction treatment doesn't work. Therefore, since it's so recalcitrant, addiction must be a disease. Therefore it's a disease just like diabetes. Therefore it can be treated. Starting from the *fact* that addiction *has not been* successfully 'treated', we arrive at the *conclusion* that addiction *can* be successfully treated.

5

Where the Disease Model Came From

If these men would addict their palates to the
pure fountains, and not wander after every polluted
stream . . .

  Oldenberg (1667)

The disease model of drug addiction was invented as a way of
describing 'alcoholism' (heavy drinking). It has since been
extended to apply to all other drugs.

The view that alcoholism is a progressive disease, the chief
symptom of which is loss of control over drinking behavior, and
whose only remedy is abstinence from all alcoholic beverages, is
about 200 years old (Levine 1978, p. 143).

During these last two centuries, public attitudes toward alcoholism have gone through three main stages. Heavy drinking was
attributed first to the drinker's will and interaction with the social
environment, then (with the Temperance movement) to alcohol
itself; and finally (with the end of Prohibition and the rise of
Alcoholics Anonymous) to the physiology of the drinker.

The 'Good Creature of God'

In colonial America the notion of alcoholism was unknown. "'Addicted' meant habituated, and one was habituated to drunkenness, not to liquor" (Levine 1978, p. 147). The Puritan Cotton Mather called alcohol the "good creature of God." Ministers and physicians encouraged its wide use. Alcohol was considered a panacea for psychological and physical ailments.

New England's Puritan ministers praised alcohol but denounced drunkenness as a sinful and willful misuse of the 'Good Creature' (Levine 1984, p. 110). No one claimed that the drink or the body of the drinker caused habituation to drunkenness. Drinking problems were often thought to result from bad company and other forms of social interaction (Levine 1978; see also Fingarette 1988). Frequently, certain taverns were blamed.

A more hostile stance toward habitual drunkenness gradually developed, based in religious thinking. Puritan writings on the subject at the end of the seventeenth and beginning of the eighteenth century show a change. Cotton Mather began referring to drunkenness as "this engine of the Devil." His father, Increase Mather, attributed the difficulty of giving up the habit of drunkenness to "sin" (Levine 1978).

Terms such as 'craving' and 'overwhelming desire', often heard today in connection with the twentieth-century concept of loss of control, were not used to explain the colonial drunkard's 'sinful' habit. The sin that caused the habit was the drunkard's "love of 'excess' drink to the point of drunkenness. . . . Drunkenness was a choice, albeit a sinful one, which some individuals make" (Levine 1978, pp. 148–49).

These were interactionist and moralistic views of drunkenness. People considered drunkenness a natural behavior, as natural as any excessive pursuit of pleasure. Such attitudes prevailed until the mid-eighteenth century, when physicians began to look for distinctions among different kinds of desire and will, categorizing some as natural and some as diseased. Medical explanations for 'unnatural' or deviant behavior emerged (Levine 1978; Grob 1981).

A Disease Is Invented

Benjamin Rush, a leader among eighteenth-century physicians came up with a new way of defining drunken deviance in 1774. He declared it a disease—a disease of the will. Levine identifies four new contributions in Rush's approach:

> First, he identified the causal agent—spirituous liquors; second, he clearly described the drunkard's condition as loss of control over drinking behavior—as compulsive activity; third, he declared the condition to be a disease; and fourth, he prescribed total abstinence as the only way to cure the drunkard. (Levine 1978, p. 152)

Rush's writings marked a major shift in beliefs about drunkenness. Similar ideas appeared at the same time in the writings of the physician Thomas Trotter of Edinburgh, where Rush had received his medical degree:

> In medical language, I consider drunkenness, strictly speaking, to be a disease; produced by a remote cause, and giving birth to actions and movements in the living body, that disorder the functions of health. (Trotter 1813, p. B2)

Neither Rush nor Trotter offered scientific evidence to support this new claim, but Rush was a powerful rhetorician and exerted an influence on public opinion (Szasz 1970; Levine 1978). The newly invented medical language grew to be accepted as fact. The 'good creature of God' had become the 'Demon Rum' (Szasz 1970; Levine 1978; Blumberg 1978; Fingarette 1988; Blumberg and Pittman 1991).

.   A curious union of moralism and medicine gained momentum during this period. Health and wealth became synonymous with temperance, and disease with intemperance, as illustrated by Rush's "moral and physical thermometer" (Rush 1981). The thermometer, a figure in Rush's original text, was "a scale of the progress of Temperance and Intemperance—Liquors with effects in their usual order." Rush assigned water the highest temperature, followed by milk and 'small' beer. These, Rush associated with "serenity of mind, reputation, long life, & happiness." Cider, perry, wine, porter, and strong beer appeared in succession down the thermometer with increasingly "cold" temperatures and were said to produce "cheerfulness, strength, and nourishment, when taken only in small quantities, and at meals." Finally, a variety of hard liquors of the time occupied the area below zero. These, Rush claimed, would result in various vices, diseases, and other evil consequences.

Rush believed that because spirits were no longer primarily used medicinally by physicians, but had become a beverage used by the general population, new diseases had appeared as well as new symptoms of old diseases. He came to believe that in general spirits were neither necessary nor useful under any circumstances. They were undesirable to society and a threat to the Republic. He predicted that "a people corrupted with strong drink cannot long be a *free* people, for the use of spirituous liquors will corrupt the rules of the community and so corrupt the laws that they make" (Blumberg and Pittman 1991, pp. 31–32). These were moral judgments and proclamations disguised in medical language. As Szasz has noted, "Rush did not recognize that drinking was a medical problem; he defined it as one" (1970, p. 141).

From Rush's time until the repeal of Prohibition, alcohol was regarded as a *universally* addictive substance capable of corrupting and thereby 'diseasing' any person, regardless of their prior moral standing. Thus, the blame for alcohol-related problems shifted from 'bad company' to the beverage itself. Alcohol became viewed as a panapathogen, a source of all problems. Rush asserted that abstinence was the only way to treat the disease of alcoholism. For many people, abstinence came to mean coerced abstinence—legal prohibition.

Universal Addictiveness

The concept of temperance was ambiguous in the early days of the Temperance Movement. Before Rush, temperance meant moderation, or control, in the drinking of beer and wine and abstinence in relation to distilled liquors (Levine 1984). Rush advocated abstinence from all alcohol. Leaders of the Temperance Movement acclaimed Rush as their inspiration. His writings on the relationship between intemperance and ardent spirits, his descriptions of the individual and social consequences of the use of liquor, as well as his recommendation of total abstinence, formed part of the essential core of 'temperance' ideology throughout the nineteenth century (Levine 1978, p. 153).

The new idea that drunkards could not control their drinking spread through public testimonials. "By about the mid-1830s, certain assumptions about the inner experience of the drunkard had become central to temperance thought. The desire for alcohol was seen as 'overpowering,' and frequently labeled a disease" (Levine 1978, p. 154).

The view of temperance advocates was not purely medical: to them drunkenness was both a sin and a disease. It began as a sin— the choice to be drunk repeatedly—and became a disease (Levine 1978, p. 157). Good morals, which in relation to alcohol meant abstinence, protected individuals from getting the disease and cured them if they had succumbed. Thus, moralism was an important element in the first efforts to define alcoholism as a disease.

Temperance activists despised moderate drinkers more than habitual drunkards, who were objects of compassion and altruism. We might speculate that temperance enthusiasts felt uneasy about the phenomenon of moderate drinking. Moderate drinkers exercised discretion and autonomy; they controlled their drinking through exercise of their willpower. In so doing they continually exhibited a practical refutation of Temperance leaders' claims that alcohol destroyed the will.

For members of the Temperance movement, the belief that alcohol, an environmental agent, and "wrong morals" were the causes of drunkenness disease served to justify a paternalistic approach. Since no one could resist becoming a drunk if they imbibed alcohol, heavy drinkers had no choice and could be helped only by making alcohol unavailable.

The mix of moralism and medicine gained a legal foothold, beginning with Prohibition. Paternalism and public health ideology became deeply enmeshed and have remained so to the present day. Prohibition was the result of a shift of focus in the Temperance Movement from *assimilative* to *coercive* reform. The original aim of absorbing sinners into the 'sanctuary of the flock' became a campaign to overpower the forces of evil represented by alcohol.

The champion of assimilative reform viewed the drinker as part of a social system in which the reformer's culture was dominant. On this assumption his invitation to the drinker to reform made sense. The champion of coercive reform cannot make this assumption. He sees the object of reform as someone who rejects the social dominance of the reformer and denies the legitimacy of his life style. Since the dominance of his culture and the social status of his group are denied, the coercive reformer turns to law and force as ways to affirm it. (Gusfield 1963, p. 7)

Medical rhetoric was used to achieve these ends. According to Bakalar and Grinspoon:

> The campaign against alcohol, like other antidrug campaigns, was also a movement for public health reform. Often parallels were drawn between drunkenness and cholera, the most terrifying epidemic disease of the nineteenth century; like cholera, alcohol abuse was regarded as a symptom of social disorder as well as a disease—something that required indirect solutions. The teaching of physiology and hygiene in public schools was promoted mainly by temperance reformers and prohibitionists; much more space in school textbooks was devoted to the dangers of alcohol in the 1880s than in the 1930s. (Sometimes lurid misinformation was introduced into this educational material—for example, the assertion that alcohol could burn the throat or cause spontaneous combustion in a drunkard. Parallels with more recent antidrug campaigns are evident.) (1984, p. 83)

From Demon Rum to Alcoholics Anonymous

In 1919, political lobbying for temperance culminated in Prohibition, with ratification of the Eighteenth Amendment. The Volstead Act gave Congress and the states the power to enforce the amendment, which prohibited the manufacture, transportation, and sale of alcoholic beverages.

The incidence of, and problems associated with, heavy drinking decreased during Prohibition (Musto 1987; Bakalar and Grinspoon, 1984), although not necessarily because of it (Levine 1984). However, the law was only very imperfectly enforced. A new arena of criminal activity emerged in connection with the illegal distribution of alcohol. People began to object to the crime and other problems caused by the illegality of alcohol. Some business interests gave generously in support of repeal, partly because it was believed that repeal would result in a higher liquor tax and thereby reduce taxation on personal income. There was also a fear that "disrespect for prohibition was producing widespread disrespect for all law including property law" (Levine 1984, p. 115).

Prohibition was repealed in 1933. Repeal decriminalized alcoholism. Subsequently, it became medicalized (Cahalan 1988).

Once again, public attitudes about drinking changed. Most people did not subscribe to the temperance propaganda that alcohol was a universally addictive substance. Many people obviously drank without problems and believed they had a right to drink. The idea of free will in relation to alcohol re-emerged. Temperance beliefs about alcohol lost their popularity, but alongside the free-will philosophy, the concept of alcoholism as a medical condition persisted.

The resolution of this tension would be to accept that most people could drink moderately without losing their free will, but to assert that a minority of people, because of something in their bodies, were incapable of drinking any alcohol without becoming enslaved to it.

A new disease model was given wide dissemination in 1935 with the founding and remarkable growth of Alcoholics Anonymous (AA), a self-help spiritual fellowship of recovering alcoholics committed to helping one another maintain sobriety (Leach and Norris 1977; Kurtz 1988).

AA was very much a child of the Temperance movement. Levine points out that we now tend to think of the Temperance movement as "condemnatory and unsympathetic to the inebriate." In reality, "temperance supporters were the most sympathetic and helpful and are the true forerunners of both Alcoholics Anonymous and of most contemporary forms of alcoholism treatment. (Levine 1984, p. 112)

Unlike their Temperance predecessors, however, the founders of AA acknowledged that most people can drink alcohol without becoming addicted.

> Following the teachings of Dr. William Silkworth, Wilson and Smith [the founders of AA] maintained that people who became alcoholics had a disease—they had something wrong with their bodies which eventually made them unable to control their drinking . . .The brilliantly original contribution of the founders of Alcoholic Anonymous was to marry this 'new disease conception' to a remarkable organizational form: a self-help network of 'recovered' alcoholics who frankly discussed their drinking and their lives, who helped each other to stay off alcohol, who went to other alcoholics offering help and a program that worked to maintain sobriety, and improve one's life, and who did this 'anonymously'. (Levine 1984, p. 116)

AA founders Wilson and Smith held that alcohol was addicting for a small percentage of the general population. This is still the view held by many people, and today is often estimated at 10 percent (Cahalan 1970). (I have frequently observed that when people want to pull a 'minority' percentage out of the air, with absolutely no facts to go on, they usually come up with 10 percent.)

Physiological differences shared by 'alcoholics' allegedly prevented them from being able to drink in a responsible manner. For them, 'prohibition' in the form of complete abstinence from alcoholic beverages was still the only way to control their drinking behavior (see also Donovan 1984; Miller and Mahler 1991).

With the rise of AA, the location of the source of addiction had been changed. As Levine says,

> The Temperance Movement found the source of addiction in the drug itself—alcohol was viewed as an inherently addicting substance, much as heroin is today. Post-Prohibition thought locates the source of addiction in the individual body—only some people, it is argued, for reasons yet unknown, become addicted to alcohol. (1978, p. 144)

The Loss-of-Control Theory

In the 1940s the AA paradigm found new support in the work of E.M. Jellinek at Yale University (Jellinek 1946; 1952). Influenced by AA, he described behavioral patterns of drinking similar to those reported by AA. He wrote of specific stages in the development of drinking which he characterized by Greek letters (1960). He named one group of alcoholics "gamma" types and claimed they suffered from loss of control in their drinking behavior.

Loss of control refers to the alleged power of one drink of alcohol to set in motion a physiological chain reaction within some alcoholics that deprives them of volitional control over drinking. This concept became the cornerstone of the modern disease concept of alcoholism and of other addictions as well (see also Keller 1972; 1976; 1982; Ludwig and Wikler 1974).

> Recovered alcoholics in Alcoholics Anonymous speak of 'loss of control' to denote that stage in the development of their drinking history when the ingestion of one alcoholic drink sets up a chain reaction so that they are unable to adhere to their intention to 'have one or two drinks only' but continue to ingest more and more—often with quite some difficulty and disgust—contrary to their volition. (Jellinek 1960, p. 41)

Similarities between Rush and Jellinek have also been noted:

> Rush's Thermometer . . . [was] strikingly similar in purpose and form
> to such later illustrations as E.M. Jellinek's graph . . . of the phases of
> alcohol addiction. . . . The illustrations from both eras explained alco-
> holism as a progressive and cumulative process, through which alco-
> holics passed in a generally predictable sequence of steps. In all these
> illustrations, clearly defined stages of problem drinking had corre-
> sponding social and physical consequences (Lender and Karnchanapee
> 1977, pp. 1354–360).

The Selling of the Disease Concept

The modern 'alcoholism movement' came into being through
intense public relations campaigns by members of AA (in particu-
lar, by Marty Mann, an early member of AA and founder of the
National Council on Alcoholism), and by the Yale Center of Alcohol
Studies, the Center of Alcohol Studies, Rutgers University, E.M.
Jellinek, Mark Keller (editor of the *Quarterly Journal of Studies on
Alcohol*), and Selden Bacon (Levine 1984).

In 1954 these campaigns scored a signal triumph when the
American Medical Association accepted alcoholism as a disease
characterized by loss-of-control behavior (AMA 1967; see also
Criteria Committee, National Council on Alcoholism 1972; Cahalan
1988). The idea seemed to take hold much more slowly among the
general population. By 1964 there was "little solid evidence of the
degree of public acceptance of the illness concept, or of its attitu-
dinal and behavioral correlates" (Mulford and Miller 1964; Verden
et al. 1969). The American Medical Association issued the following statement in 1967:

> Alcoholism is an illness characterized by preoccupation with alcohol
> and loss of control over its consumption such as to lead usually to
> intoxication if drinking is begun; by chronicity; by progression; and by
> tendency toward relapse. It is typically associated with physical dis-
> ability and impaired emotional, occupational, and/or social adjust-
> ments as a direct consequence of persistent and excessive use. (p. 6)

Numerous medical and psychiatric associations around the
world soon followed the AMA in adopting the disease theory of
alcoholism.

Twelve-Step Imperialism

In the nineteenth century, American consumption of opiates, as of alcohol, was considerably higher than it has been in the twentieth. Opiates were completely legal, and very widely used. Laudanum, opium dissolved in an alcoholic drink, was widely employed to quieten infants and as an all-purpose pain-reliever. Benjamin Franklin consumed laudanum regularly in the final years of his life, to reduce the pain from his kidney stones. Use of opiates increased steadily throughout the century. A new form of morphine, heroin, was marketed by Bayer in 1898, as an effective pain-killer. Narcotics were freely available from mail-order catalogs such as Sears, Roebuck. The growing use of the hypodermic syringe was at first seen as lessening the 'danger' of 'addiction'.

Over time opiates became purer, and cocaine too was purified, providing a more concentrated effect than the traditional ingestion of coca leaves by mouth. Coca-cola was launched in 1886 as an alternative to the popular 'cocaine wines'. Coca-cola was thus a temperance beverage: it offered the supposedly riskless benefits of cocaine without the temptation of the demon alcohol. Cocaine was removed from Coca-cola in 1900, anticipating the passage of laws restricting cocaine availability to doctor's prescription.

Around the end of the nineteenth century, fears grew of 'addiction' and of other alleged side effects, fueled mainly by horrific anecdotal accounts (see Musto 1987; Musto apparently accepts all these anecdotes as justified; no doubt many of them were). Opinion was rapidly turned around, opiate and cocaine use began to fall sharply, and narcotics were first legally controlled nationwide in the Harrison Act of 1914. Soon cocaine was a thing of the past for most Americans, and attention was focussed on the bigger perceived danger of alcohol. By the time narcotics had re-emerged as a major issue, the new disease model of alcoholism, incorporating the spiritual thinking of AA, had been extended to other drug addictions. The ruling ideology has yet to acknowledge that most people can consume narcotics without any danger of 'addiction'. Aside from that, the entire 'treatment industry' is now dominated by AA's Twelve-Step thinking.

6

Smoking Right and Responsibility

Each man to what sport and revels his addiction leads
him.
       William Shakespeare, *Othello*

The increasing attempt to hold tobacco companies responsible for
the consequences of smoking behavior poses a greater threat to liberty in a free society than nicotine ever could (Hansen 1997).
Despite the fact that addiction is not listed in standard textbooks of
pathology (because it does not meet the nosological criteria for disease classification), anti-smoking propagandists define the behavior of smokers as if it were some kind of epileptic seizure. Their
attempts to absolve people of responsibility for their behavior are
the obvious consequence. Yet attributing smoking to involuntary
'addiction' is not supported by the facts and has inevitably led to a
legal policy based on fiction.

    There's a difference between what smoking does to a person's
body and how smoke gets into his body. The U.S. Food and Drug
Administration (FDA), in co-operation with the public-health
industry and with attorneys who argue that smokers get sick
because they have 'lost the ability to choose' not to smoke, clouds
that distinction. Concurrently, these groups suggest that a person's
body (as opposed to the person himself) causes a particular vice

and its consequences, that is, smoking behavior doesn't exist apart from physiological processes. Nothing could be further from the truth.

While their intentions may be compassionate, the net effect of their thinking is to reduce human beings to machines—chemical and electrical interactions, soul-less animals—lacking free will and moral agency, the very qualities we characterize as distinctly human. And remember machines don't operate by themselves. They're operated by people.

Does a car 'drive' the driver? Does a pencil 'write' the writer? Does a body 'run' the person? Of course not. People run their bodies, not the other way around. Yet those who assert that nicotine addiction causes smoking are engaging in just such muddleheaded thinking.

Consider the dangerous legal precedent that could be set by accepting such thinking: If smokers' physical addiction to nicotine causes them to smoke, one might just as easily argue rapists' bodies cause them to commit rape, murderers' bodies cause them to commit murder, child abusers' bodies cause them to abuse. What kind of world would we live in if those theories were upheld by the courts? If we attribute responsibility for the harm people do to themselves to physiological processes, don't we, to apply the rule of law justly, then have to remove people's responsibility for the harm they cause to others? And then we surely ought to remove moral agency and responsibility for good behaviors too: Heroism, courage and other virtuous acts such as loving and praying, academic achievement and creativity would all have to be viewed as having nothing to do with ethically-motivated human action. They would all be viewed simply as products of biology.

That's exactly the kind of argument used by people who are suing tobacco companies for injuries the plaintiffs may have caused themselves by smoking. Tobacco caused them to smoke, they claim, as if tobacco had a will of its own. Cigarettes, renamed 'nicotine-delivery systems' by the FDA (though it's not the nicotine that causes the injuries), render smokers incapable of abstinence. Any reasons for smoking thereby become irrelevant.

This doublespeak contradicts the scientific evidence: smokers quit all the time—when it's important to them to do so. They moderate their smoking at will too. For example, a study of over 5,000 Minnesota workers published in the September 1996 issue of the

American Journal of Public Health showed "a substantial proportion of smokers are low-rate users" and suggests that this proportion may be rising (Hennrikus, Jeffery, and Lando 1996). This finding supports the idea that psychological factors play a part in smokers' decisions to smoke or not to smoke. It contradicts the claim that people become physiologically enslaved by nicotine addiction once they start smoking.

Moreover, studies published in the *Journal of the American Medical Association* have long shown smokers can quit on their own (Fiore et al. 1990; Glynn 1990). This finding undoubtedly upsets the manufacturers of nicotine patches and gum, as well as those who make money on smoking-cessation clinics and programs. These groups are addicted to making money by convincing the public that smokers cannot quit on their own, that willpower won't work. So they spread the unfounded theory that smokers have an addiction disease, caused by a physiological dependency on nicotine, one they can never manage on their own. They want the public to believe their products are necessary for curing the disease. Yet scientific studies have demonstrated that treatment programs for smoking addiction don't work for most people (Fiore et al. 1990; Glynn 1990).

Choosing to quit is a simple statement of intention. Whether people are heavy or light smokers has nothing to do with the ability to quit. The best predictor of smoking and cessation of smoking is level of education (Escobedo et al. 1990). Plaintiffs' lawyers in the numerous liability cases directed at British and American tobacco companies rely on public ignorance in order to make money. They know that less educated persons on the jury are less likely to reason out the facts and more likely to be swayed in their attitudes by 'authorities' who obscure the difference between behavior and disease.

Most of us know people who smoked for years and then quit abruptly. Their bodies had adapted to nicotine and since they chose to quit, they did. Question: What do we attribute that behavior to? Answer: the exercise of free will.

And what of people who do not want to quit? Why explain their behavior using terms such as weak will and physiological addiction? Those people simply choose to continue smoking, even if a doctor or loved one has suggested they quit. They aren't suffering from a weak will. They have an iron will: they choose to continue smoking against medical advice. And ironically, they're often the ones who later transform their iron will into an iron fist, demanding that they be financially compensated for the consequences of their own behavior.

There's nothing particularly unusual about noncompliance with medical advice or blaming others for one's own behavior. Many people continue to engage in certain behaviors against medical advice. How many people continue to eat a high-fat diet when their doctor recommends against it? If they develop cardiovascular disease, will they blame McDonald's and Burger King for hooking them on hamburgers and french fries? Why not?

Smoking and quitting, like eating and dieting or exercising and being a couch potato, are matters of free will and personal choice. Yes, habits may cause disease—but habits aren't diseases in and of themselves. Cancer is a disease. Smoking is a habitual behavior. Moreover, likening a behavior to a disease seems especially cruel to people with real diseases. A person cannot choose to quit or moderate diabetes.

The price of freedom in a free society is responsibility for the consequences of one's actions. Liberty and responsibility are positively correlated. That's a fact. People who claim addiction causes people to smoke say the two are negatively correlated. That's fiction. We cannot increase freedom by decreasing personal responsibility. That's the road to serfdom.

7

Who Are the Addiction Treatment Providers?

Some princes are addicted to others for stipends.
J. Daus (1560)

Providers of addiction treatment have a considerable influence on addiction policy, yet until recently almost nothing was known about who these people are and what they believe. To find out more, I conducted a national study of treatment providers (see the Appendix following this chapter). I believe that the individuals surveyed in my study are broadly representative of treatment providers generally.

Treatment providers are mostly:

- male (63.1 percent)
- Caucasian (94.9 percent)
- non-Christian (53.6 percent)
- married (63.4 percent)
- past (69.8 percent) or current (34.2 percent) members of Alcoholics Anonymous
- with a graduate degree (73.9 percent)
- without a medical degree (98 percent)
- certified as treatment providers (51.9 percent)

There are different kinds of addiction treatments, but almost all of them consist entirely of talking. 'Treatment' means that the addict exchanges words, either with an individual (a 'therapist') or with a group of other addicts. (A very small number of treatments also employ 'anti-drug drugs', which either cause an unpleasant physical reaction or prevent the 'high' when the 'bad' drug is taken. The fatal flaw in this approach is that addicts plan ahead. Their drug taking is purposeful, deliberate, and calculated. They aim to get the high, so they either stop taking the anti-drug drug or switch to a different 'bad' drug. Adding anti-drug-drugs to the public water supply, which some would favor, would cause drug addicts to drink only bottled water.)

Alcoholics Anonymous

I was mainly interested in how treatment providers thought, but before I go on to explain what I found, let's first look at the group known as Alcoholics Anonymous (AA). AA has been the most influential force in forming people's ideas about addiction, especially the ideas held by most addiction treatment providers.

There is a popular impression that AA 'works'—that more 'alcoholics' recover through AA than would do so without AA. There is no evidence, however, to support this popular impression. Nonetheless those who do recover, and are in AA when they do, often become fervent missionaries for AA.

AA's Twelve-Step structure has been emulated by several other groups, such as Narcotics Anonymous, Smokers Anonymous, Overeaters Anonymous, and Gamblers Anonymous, all of which share the same spiritual, theological, and therapeutic outlook. Although AA's religious orientation is not disguised (no less than six of the Twelve Steps explicitly refer to God), many of the claims about addiction made by AA have become accepted in the popular culture. Few members of the general public are aware that addiction researchers have found these claims to be unfounded, and that they spring from AA's religious doctrine, not from any factual enquiry into drinking behavior.

As anthropologist William Madsen has written: "The major force dealing with alcoholism today is Alcoholics Anonymous. All good treatment facilities and treatment programs aim at getting the patient into AA" (1988, p. 26). AA has been described as a religious-conversion experience by anthropologists, sociologists, and psychologists, as well as by the courts (Antze 1987; Luff 1989; Dolan 1988). Since the major force dealing with addiction today is AA, this means that most of what we consider secular treatment for addiction really has a lot more to do with spirituality and religious thinking than many people realize.

AA literature counsels participants to "turn their lives over to a higher power." This "higher power" can be anything (presumably Muslims, Hindus, or Zoroastrians would have no problem with AA) with one exception: it cannot be the participant's own self. An AA member must accept, as the central dogma, that he or she is absolutely helpless to give up the addiction to alcohol. Only the "higher power" can bring about recovery. Wilfullness is discouraged in AA as in many cults.

We are here discussing the alleged treatment of an alleged disease. The vital 'First Step' in the 'treatment' is to accept the claim that the only possible solution is a miracle! Does this sound as if it were 'a treatable disease, just like diabetes'?

To join AA,

> an alcoholic must admit his complete weakness and inadequacy and accept whole-heartedly the belief that to live a normal life he must be utterly dependent on a power greater than himself. In other words, he must accept the power of God as a substitute for the power of the bottle to enhance his sense of potency. God 'inspirits' him, strengthening him in place of liquor. (McClelland 1972, pp. 301–02)

AA's treatment, then, involves "the systematic manipulation of symbolic elements within an individual's life to provide a new vision of that life, and of his world" (Thune 1977, p. 88). Another writer observes that AA "effectively mobilizes the poorly understood ingredients present in increased religious involvement," and "'converts' individuals from one belief system to another. It is a paradox that a major goal of AA—a strictly moral and religious system—has been to view alcohol abuse as a medical illness, not a moral failing" (Vaillant 1983, p. 194). If the 'treatment' is to transform the patient's beliefs, isn't the 'disease' metaphorical rather than strictly medical?

Three popular books used in AA are 'approved literature' by Alcoholics Anonymous General Service Conference— *The Big Book* (AA World Services 1976), *As Bill Sees It* (AA World Services 1967), and *Came to Believe* (AA World Services 1973), a collection of anecdotes describing "the spiritual adventure of A.A. as experienced by individual members." As further evidence of spiritual thinking found in AA the following passages are presented, excerpted from *The Big Book*, the 'bible' of AA (AA World Services 1976). Note not only the relationship with God but also the relationship advocated towards self:

> The central factor of our lives today is the absolute certainty that our Creator has entered into our hearts and lives in a way which is indeed miraculous. He has commenced to accomplish those things for us which we could never do by ourselves . . . The delusion that we are like other people, or presently may be, has to be smashed . . .Whether such a person [those unable to drink moderately] can quit upon a non-spiritual basis depends upon the extent to which he has already lost the power to choose whether he will drink or not . . . Lack of power, that was our dilemma. We had to find a power by which we could live, and it had to be a *Power greater than ourselves* . . . [The Big Book's] . . . main object is to enable you to find a Power greater than yourself which will solve your problem . . . We agnostics and atheists were sticking to the idea that self-sufficiency would solve our problems . . . Our ideas did not work. But the God idea did . . . When we became alcoholics, crushed by a self-imposed crisis we could not postpone or evade, we had to fearlessly face the proposition that either God is everything or else He is nothing. God either is, or He isn't. What was our choice to be? . . . The first requirement is that we be convinced that any life run on self-will can hardly be a success . . . The alcoholic is an extreme example of self-will run riot . . . Relieve me of the bondage of self . . . Being convinced that self, manifested in various ways, was what had defeated us . . . we have been not only mentally and physically ill, we have been spiritually sick. When the spiritual malady is overcome, we straighten out mentally and physically . . . We trust infinite God rather than our finite selves . . . Faith did for us what we could not do for ourselves . . . We hope that you are convinced now that God can remove whatever self-will has blocked you off from Him . . . We ask ourselves for freedom from self-will, and are careful to make no requests for ourselves only . . .*The main thing is that he be willing to believe in a Power greater than himself and that he live by spiritual principles.* (AA World Services 1976, pp. 25, 30, 34, 45, 52, 53, 60, 62, 63, 64, 65, 68, 70, 71, 87, 93; emphasis in original)

AA: A Totemic Religion?

According to Paul Antze, AA is a totemic religion: one in which some object or animal is the central focus of the belief system and serves to hold members of a group together (Antze 1987). Alcohol is the center of the AA religon; it is both God and Devil.

What is obvious is how people in AA think that alcohol is bad; what is not so obvious is how they think it is good. In AA and other Twelve-Step programs, beverage alcohol is seen as both cause and cure of members' existential problems. As well as being the cause of their problems, alcohol is the cure, in that it brought them to AA, and thus to dependence on the higher power.

According to AA thinking, an alcoholic has a 'pride' or ego problem. As the alcoholic drinks, he thinks more and more that he is effectively God. In order to get help, as his life is falling apart, the alcoholic must 'bottom out'. Bottoming out, in which the alcoholic realizes he is 'not-God' is crucial to the conversion to AA. The alcoholic 'hits bottom' and is reduced to a state of total dependence on whatever or whoever can stop his drinking. He is then ready to turn his life over to the higher power, a being similar to the Holy Spirit.

As the convert works the Twelve Steps, he is 'sponsored' by a mentor, a sort of supervisor for what the higher power wants, until he eventually graduates to become an 'old timer'. An old timer is someone who has mastered the Twelve Steps and overcome 'the pride problem'. What I've always wondered is this: if people overcome the pride problem, shouldn't they be able to drink again?

There is in AA the idea that recovered alcoholics are God's chosen people. They believe themselves to be genetically predisposed (or predetermined) to their addiction by a biological 'marker'. Alcohol brings them to hell and then to heaven.

Treatment Providers' Organizations

Let's now look at some of the leading organizations in providing addiction treatment today:

- *Alcoholics Anonymous (AA)* is a voluntary self-help group united by a distinctive set of religious beliefs. Although I criticize its specific religious orientation and the falsehoods about addiction AA disseminates, I do admire the enterprising orientation of many AA members and their willingness to help each other without recourse to paid 'professional experts'.

- *The National Association of Alcoholism and Drug Abuse Counselors (NAADAC)* is the largest association of alcoholism and drug abuse counselors in the United States. Official statements by this organization have described addiction as a "treatable disease." The organization is also actively involved in certifying alcohol and drug counselors.

- *Rational Recovery Systems (RRS)*, founded by Jack Trimpey, is a national, secular-based alternative to AA. It expanded rapidly throughout the U.S. in the early 1990s. Official statements from this organization emphasize abstinence as the most effective way of controlling addiction. It criticizes the notion of addiction as a disease, and is often critical of AA on the grounds that AA is religious (Trimpey 1989).

  Like AA, however, Rational Recovery focuses on achieving abstinence; its proponents generally do not consider moderation or controlled drinking a realistic goal. The focus on abstinence is a disease-model belief, yet members of Rational Recovery assert that addiction isn't a disease. The findings from my study contradict the theory prevalent in Rational Recovery that secular thinking and belief in abstinence are positively correlated.

- *The Society of Psychologists in Addictive Behaviors (SPAB)*, formerly a national organization in the U.S., has now become Division 50 of the American Psychological Association.

- *Secular Organization for Sobriety (SOS)*, a self-help organization founded by James Christopher, is decidedly secular in its approach, yet its founder appears to believe quite strongly in the idea that addiction is a disease: "And for me, the answer to the question, 'Can sober alcoholics ever drink again?' is an emphatic *no*." (Christopher 1988, p. 23) "We now know . . . that alcoholics differ from nonalcoholics in key *biological* ways . . . " (Christopher 1989, p. 25) We do not "know" anything of the kind. Christopher's comment here is typical of many such remarks one hears in the addiction field, a vague gesture toward evidence that does not, in fact, exist.

- *SMART Recovery* is a self-help organization that developed in 1994 as a result of a political split with Rational Recovery over non-profit status. It is growing rapidly now, and there are perhaps more SMART groups than there are RRS ones. There appear to be few substantial philosophical differences between SMART Recovery and RRS with regard to beliefs about addiction—both organizations are avowedly secular, focus on achieving abstinence (as opposed to moderation or controlled drinking) and rely heavily on principles of cognitive therapy (SMART Recovery 1996). Both use cognitive therapy principles, that is, they focus on changing the beliefs people have about themselves and the world as a way of helping people with addiction.

SMART acknowledges the research on moderation and controlled drinking and drug use as valid, and appropriate for some people.

• *Moderation Management (MM)* is dealt with in Chapter 10 below.

AA has been the main influence on thinking about addiction, but there has been a reaction against the overtly theistic orientation of AA, leading to new self-help organizations with a more secular rhetoric. People in the more secular groups often criticize AA for its specifically religious character. These critics of AA mostly accept the disease model, and one sometimes finds them assuming that religious thinking goes along with resistance to the disease model. While this assumption is understandable, it is the exact reverse of the truth: 'religious' thinking is actually strongly associated with belief in the disease model; it is the more secular, better-educated, and more scientifically-minded people who tend to be proponents of the free-will model.

Why the Treatment Providers' Beliefs Are Important

Treatment providers are often regarded as authorities on addiction, and they gain prestige from their experience of working with addicts. For example, responding to critics of the disease model of alcoholism, Vaillant asks why

experienced alcohol workers and recovering alcoholics . . . accept the view that alcoholism is a disease? Why is it mainly less competent people, the active alcoholics, who agree with Professor Fingarette that they are just 'heavy drinkers'? (1990, p. 4)

Notice the sly use of the word 'just' to insinuate that if heavy drinking is not literally a disease, it must be simple or inconsequential. One could simply turn Vaillant's question around, and ask why an increasing number of psychologists and other highly competent people happen to agree with those active or recovered alcoholics who disagree with their treatment providers. One could also cite the fact that many alcoholics, including some of the most 'hopeless' cases, have completely swallowed the disease theory.

It's also worth observing that those with the most frequent and direct experience of some phenomenon are not always recognized as the most reliable authorities: meteorologists know more than sailors about the weather, despite the repeated confirmation of sailors' folklore by their daily experience. Since the treatment providers are in fact predominantly religious proselytizers, not disinterested enquirers, there is no need for Vaillant to be puzzled.

Qualms have often been voiced by exemplary non-radical writers about the influence of the beliefs of addiction treatment providers. For instance, a reviewer in *The New England Journal of Medicine* mentioned the possibility that treatment providers might be "in a self-interested position to maintain a belief in a psychologically unsophisticated model of disease" (Dodes 1992, p. 1369). On a different tack, an editorial in the *British Journal of Addiction* raised the question of research which cast doubt on the "*belief* among personnel and clients that alcoholism is a disease involving 'loss of' or 'impaired control' over the intake of alcohol" (Bergmakr and Oscarsson 1991; emphasis in original). This was a problem for the editorial writer, who supposed that belief in these false notions could in effect be therapeutic.

As a framework for investigating the beliefs of treatment providers, I used the free-will model and the disease model. The free-will model conceives addiction as a choice. Here human action is considered the function of moral agency and psychological motivation. The disease model conceives addiction as an involuntary activity, characterized by loss of control. Here behavior is considered to be caused and determined by forces external to the self.

It is logically conceivable that people could maintain addiction is involuntary yet not a disease or that they could hold addiction to be a disease, but with the addict able to control the addictive behavior. In practice, however, it is very rare to encounter either of these combinations. Virtually all the claims that addiction is involuntary stem from disease-model thinking.

'Free-will' is used in its everyday, rather than philosophical, sense. Acceptance of the free-will model does not require taking a position on the philosophical question of free-will and determinism. A determinist could accept the free-will model, as long as the determinist recognized a practical distinction between voluntary and involuntary human action (which most determinists do). One can therefore think of the 'free-will' model as 'the free choice model' or simply 'the choice model'.

Facts about Treatment Providers

As a rule, the more spiritual-thinking addiction-treatment providers have been in AA. The strength of their spiritual thinking depends in part on how many years they spent in AA. They also tend to think of themselves as addicts (alcoholics) in recovery. Even if they weren't in AA when they completed my survey, if they had been in AA in the past they tend to be spiritual thinkers (as compared to those treatment providers who were not in AA in the past).

Addiction-treatment providers who are abstinent tend to be spiritual thinkers more than those who drink alcohol or consume drugs. The lower the educational status of addiction-treatment providers, the stronger their spiritual thinking. Addiction-treatment providers who are certified tend to engage in spiritual thinking more than those providers who are not certified (which is not surprising, as the exams for certification basically test whether you know and can assent to the disease model).

Female providers are more spiritual thinking than male providers. Members of NAADAC tend to be the strongest spiritual thinkers, followed by members of SPAB (now Division 50 of the APA), and then RRS. Catholics tend to believe more strongly in a supernatural power that can influence personal experience compared to Protestants, followed by those who are Jewish, agnostic, atheistic, and of 'other denominations'.

Treatment providers who believe addiction is a choice are more likely to reject the idea that a metaphysical power can influence personal experience. They are not usually in AA, are not generally certified as addiction-treatment providers, and tend to be male. They are also more likely to be members of RRS.

It usually comes as a surprise to those outside the field that secular-minded, non-religious people tend to reject the disease model while traditionally religious people tend to accept it. Isn't belief in the disease model a progressive, scientific way of thinking? And isn't belief in personal volition and individual responsibility an old-fashioned notion you might expect to be associated with traditional religion?

Although the 'scientistic' belief that the body somehow controls the mind may be prevalent among progressive-minded secular intellectuals, and may explain why they have tended to surrender without a fight to the disease theory promoted by a specific kind of religious thinking, the fact that religion, not science, is the source of the disease model has left its mark. A key fact is that most addiction treatment providers have themselves been in AA. They are themselves recovered addicts (alcoholics) who have probably undergone a conversion experience to the peculiar AA world-view, and see it as their mission in life to propagandize for this world-view at every opportunity.

There seem to be two conflicting strains in Christian thinking: that we have to 'work out our salvation in fear and trembling' and that we are completely powerless and can do nothing for ourselves except submit to the Holy Spirit. The latter strain is the one emphasized by the offshoot of Moral Re-Armament, itself a strange offshoot of Protestantism, which took the form of AA.

One exceptional combination of spiritual thinking and the free-will model approach is voiced by William L. Playfair, M.D. Playfair argues against the disease model of addiction from a fundamentalist Christian perspective and stresses the idea that addiction is a sin (Playfair 1991):

> There are two primary reasons I oppose sending the non-Christian to the recovery industry. He will be told his sin is a sickness; he will never be confronted with his real and most basic moral and spiritual problem. And he will more than likely be introduced to the *any god* of Twelve Stepdom, who is, by Biblical criteria, a false god.
>
> These are the very same reasons I oppose utilizing the recovery industry for Christians. (pp. 174–75)

Playfair draws on the writings of secular critics of the disease model to help support his theological perspective on addiction.

Playfair is unusual. Generally speaking, the Christian churches have completely succumbed to the doctrines of 'mental health' and 'addiction treatment' (Farber 1999). Jerry Falwell, a respected Baptist pastor, has authoritatively stated that Bill Clinton is suffering from the illness of sex addiction and requires professional counseling. As a neutral observer who is neither an evangelical Protestant nor a believer in the religion of 'mental health', I find it fascinating that Reverend Falwell appears completely unaware that he is embracing the doctrines of a rival religion. Would Reverend Falwell be so similarly ecumenical as to say that Clinton suffers from bad karma and will be reincarnated as a billy goat?

AA Spiritual Thinking: Kurtz's Four Elements

Kurtz analyzed AA in 1988 and describes four elements in the stories told by AA members which are "the primary way in which sobriety, or spirituality, is not only transmitted but grown into" in AA (O'Connell 1991). Kurtz calls these spiritual elements 'release', 'gratitude', 'humility', and 'tolerance' (O'Connell 1991; E. Kurtz, personal communication, January 2nd, 1992; Kurtz and Ketcham 1992). 'Release' pertains to truth-telling. 'Gratitude' refers to the unearned 'gift' from God of release from alcoholism. 'Tolerance' refers to the appreciation of individual differences among AA group members. 'Humility' refers to the telling of one's story or experience of trouble in life, particularly with alcohol.

According to Kurtz,

> more than any other person, the alcoholic has come close to discovering magic. For the alcoholic, alcohol *is* magic. In recovery, once the person ceases to realize that recovery is miracle and there is an air of mystery to it, and starts seeking the magic, almost certainly such a person will go back to the booze because nothing is as magical as alcohol is to the alcoholic. (O'Connell 1991, p. 2; emphasis in original)

Here are some references in AA literature to each of the four spiritual elements identified by Kurtz. They all refer to God or the higher power, and they are all characterized by the 'spiritual' qualities of 'miracle' and 'mystery'. The statements have been slightly modified from AA literature to improve clarity (adapted from

Alcoholics Anonymous World Services 1967; 1973; 1976; Kurtz 1988).

Release

Two examples of spiritual statements characterized by *release* are the following: "My 'higher power' has mysteriously accomplished those things in my life which I could never do by myself." "I got positive results in my life when I laid aside prejudice and expressed a willingness to believe in a Power greater than myself, even though it is impossible for me to fully define or comprehend that Power, which is God."

Gratitude

Two examples characterized by *gratitude* are the following: "The central factor of my life today is the absolute certainty that my Creator has entered into my heart and life in a way which is indeed miraculous." "When I make right decisions in my life I believe it is important to thank God for giving me the courage and the grace to act in this way."

Humility

Two examples characterized by *humility* are: "First of all, in order to begin solving my problems, I had to quit playing God. I had to realize that I was not God." (According to Kurtz, the idea that the alcoholic is not God pervades all AA philosophy and literature.) "I seek through prayer and meditation to improve my conscious contact with God as I understand Him, praying only for knowledge of His will and the power to carry that out."

Tolerance

Finally, two examples exhibiting *tolerance*: "I believe that people who have done wrong to me are perhaps spiritually sick. I think it is best to ask God to help me show them the same tolerance, pity, and patience that I should give to a sick friend." "I have no desire to convince anyone that there is only one way by which faith can be acquired. All of us, whatever our race, creed, color, or beliefs, are the children of a living Creator, with whom we may form a simple, understandable relationship, as soon as we are willing enough to try."

The Two Dimensions of AA Spiritual Thinking

Contrary to Kurtz, I maintain that there are just two 'dimensions' of AA spiritual thinking, and I believe my statistical study bears this out. One dimension incorporates spiritual beliefs characterized by release, gratitude, and humility. The second dimension incorporates spiritual beliefs characterized by tolerance.

In other words, release, gratitude, humility are so strongly associated in AA thinking that they count as one element or 'dimension'. In my statistical results, these three were positively correlated with one another, while the 'tolerance' dimension was more distinct.

The statement "I feel it is important to thank God when I manage to do the right thing" is most representative of the three dimensions of release, gratitude, and humility. It contains clear indications of release and humility, in addition to gratitude. For example, 'doing the right thing' can be interpreted as a release from doing the wrong things. 'Thanking God' for something the individual does that is considered good is a form of humility. So, from a logical point of view, it makes sense that the three dimensions would group together here.

Appendix: A Study of Addiction Treatment Providers

How the Study Was Conducted

A total of 511 seven-page surveys with cover letter were mailed to addiction-treatment providers in the U.S., Canada, and Australia.

Two hundred surveys were distributed to a random sample of members of NAADAC, the largest association of alcoholism and drug abuse counselors in the United States.

One hundred forty-four surveys were mailed to the complete list of treatment providers serving as supervisors for Rational Recovery Systems (RRS) groups.

One hundred sixty-seven surveys were mailed to addiction-treatment providers who were members of SPAB. The secretary/treasurer of SPAB hand-picked these members on the basis of their having listed themselves as treatment providers. SPAB's orientation to addiction was unknown.

These three organizations were chosen to represent a diversity of beliefs. While other organizations of treatment providers exist, these groups were selected on the basis of suspected diversity and accessibility.

Completed and returned surveys totaled 327, constituting an initial 64 percent return rate. Of these, 32 respondents indicated they were not addiction-treatment providers; therefore, 295 providers established the primary sample studied; 58 percent of those sent a survey. One hundred four surveys were returned from NAADAC (52 percent of those mailed to this group); 98 surveys were returned from SPAB (59 percent of those mailed); and 91 surveys were returned from RRS (63 percent of those mailed).

The Addiction Belief Scale

I developed a new scale in my study to find out what people believe about addiction. This scale consisted of 18 statements representing beliefs regarding the meaning of drug addiction and addicts' ability to control their addiction (Table 1). These items served in one part

Table 1. The Addiction Belief Scale

A1. Most addicts don't know they have a problem and must be forced to recognize they are addicts. [Disease model]

A2. Addicts cannot control themselves when they drink or take drugs. [Disease model]

A3. The only solution to drug addiction and/or alcoholism is treatment. [Disease model]

A4. The best way to overcome addiction is by relying on your own willpower. [free-will model]

A5. Addiction is an all-or-nothing disease: A person cannot be a temporary drug addict with a mild drinking or drug problem. [Disease model]

A6. People can stop relying on drugs or alcohol as they develop new ways to deal with life. [free-will model]

A7. Addiction has more to do with the environments people live in than the drugs they are addicted to. [free-will model]

A8. People often outgrow drug and alcohol addiction. [free-will model]

A9. The most important step in overcoming an addiction is to acknowledge that you are powerless and can't control it. [Disease model]

A10. Abstinence is the only way to control alcoholism/drug addiction. [Disease model]

A11. Physiology, not psychology, determines whether one drinker will become addicted to alcohol and another will not. [Disease model]

A12. Alcoholics and drug addicts can learn to moderate their drinking or cut down on their drug use. [free-will model]

A13. People become addicted to drugs/alcohol when life is going badly for them. [free-will model]

A14. The fact that alcoholism runs in families means that it is a genetic disease. [Disease model]

A15. You have to rely on yourself to overcome an addiction such as alcoholism. [free-will model]

A16. Drug addicts and alcoholics can find their own ways out of addiction, without outside help, given the opportunity. [free-will model]

A17. People who are drug addicted can never outgrow addiction and are always in danger of relapsing. [Disease model]

A18. Drug addiction is a way of life people rely on to cope with the world. [free-will model]

Note. The highest possible score is 90. The higher the score, the stronger the belief in the disease model of addiction. The lower the score, the stronger the belief in the free-will model of addiction.

of my study as what is called the criterion. They represent the two perspectives on addiction. The statements representing the two perspectives are marked by brackets in Table 1.

People in the study were asked to mark the extent to which they agreed or disagreed with each statement along a five-point Likert scale ranging from 'strongly disagree' to 'strongly agree'. The higher the degree of belief in the disease model of addiction, the higher their total score.

The highest possible score for each item was 5, and for all 18 items, 90. The conceptual median score was 45. The strongest possible belief in the free-will model of addiction is represented by a score of 5 for each of the nine free-will items and zero for each of the nine disease-model items (or a total of 45). Table 2 shows the mean scores on the ABS for addiction-treatment providers.

The Spiritual Belief Scale

Since spiritual thinking is such an important part of AA and related self-help programs, and the disease model of addiction found rebirth in AA, I decided to create a new scale to measure spiritual thinking based on AA philosophy. The second part of the survey I mailed out, the Spiritual Belief Scale (SBS) (Table 3), included eight items measuring spiritual thinking. These items were adapted from AA after an exhaustive analysis of AA literature. Note how each contains a reference to God or "spiritual health." The items are grouped according to the analysis of four spiritual characteristics of AA identified by Ernest Kurtz, considered by many people who believe in the disease model of alcoholism as a scholar of AA (Kurtz 1988; O'Connell 1991; Kurtz and Ketcham 1992).

'Spiritual thinking' is a broad term. Its use as a dependent variable in my study was defined in terms of how it occurs in the philosophy of AA, and is thereby related to beliefs regarding addiction (Bales 1944; Tiebout 1953; Stewart 1955; Trice 1957; 1959; Cohen 1962; Eckhardt 1967; Donovan 1984).

Table 2. Mean Scores for the Addiction Belief Scale (ABS)

	Mean	SD	n	p
ABS	54.12	13.55	295	
Gender				<.01
Males	50.91	13.69	186	
Females	59.60	11.43	109	
Professional Group				<.01
NAADAC	64.97	08.81	104	
SPAB	52.88	10.95	98	
RRS	42.89	10.71	91	
Religious affiliation				<.01
Protestant	57.94	12.91	81	
Catholic	58.70	11.51	46	
Jewish	54.98	10.04	42	
Atheist	38.64	10.39	22	
Agnostic	45.73	12.48	30	
Other	54.63	13.76	64	
Certified?				<.01
Yes	57.44	13.10	153	
No	50.54	13.15	142	
In recovery?				<.01
Yes	61.71	11.87	100	
No	50.36	12.70	193	
In AA now?				<.01
Yes	64.43	09.37	101	
No	48.75	12.23	194	
In AA in the past?				<.01
Yes	56.47	13.61	206	
No	48.08	11.57	80	
Abstinent?				<.01
Yes	58.00	12.90	182	
No	47.74	12.02	111	
Recovery beliefs	25.07	24.42	293	

Note. The highest possible score is 90. The higher the score, the stronger the belief in the disease model of addiction. The lower the score, the stronger the belief in the free-will model.

Table 3. The Spiritual Belief Scale (SBS)

S1. I feel that in many ways turning my life over to God has actually set me free. [Release]

S2. I know that all the best things in my life have come to me through God. [Release]

S3. I believe I am blessed by God with many gifts I don't deserve. [Gratitude]

S4. I feel it is important to thank God when I manage to do the right thing. [Gratitude]

S5. It's only when I stop trying to play God that I can begin to learn what God wants for me. [Humility]

S6. I know I am able to meet life's challenges only with God's help. [Humility]

S7. I know that forgiving those who have hurt me is important for my spiritual health. [Tolerance]

S8. I believe there are many ways to know God and that my way is not the only way. [Tolerance]

Note. The highest possible score is 40. The higher the score, the stronger the belief in a metaphysical power that can influence personal experience, that is, spiritual thinking.

Again, participants in the study were asked to mark the extent to which they agreed or disagreed with each of the statements in the SBS along a five-point Likert scale ranging from 'strongly disagree' to 'strongly agree'. The SBS was scored in the direction of high spiritual belief, that is, the higher the score, the more the participants tend to engage in spiritual thinking along the dimensions described.

Demographic Characteristics of Addiction-Treatment Providers

The average age of participants in this study was 44 years. The average number of years participants spent in AA was 5.04 years. One hundred seventeen participants indicated they had spent no time in AA.

Two hundred eight addiction-treatment providers were Caucasian (94.9 percent), seven were African-American (2.4 percent), four were Hispanic (one percent), three were American Indian (one percent) and one was Asian (0.3 percent). Forty one providers were never married (13.9 percent), 187 were married (63.4 percent), six were widowed (two percent), and 59 were separated or divorced (20 percent). Twenty eight providers indicated

Table 4. Demographic Characteristics of the Sample

	SPAB	RRS	NAADAC	n	(%)
Gender					
Male	63 (64.0)	69 (76.0)	53 (51.0)	186	(63.1)
Female	35 (36.0)	22 (24.0)	51 (49.0)	109	(36.9)
In recovery?					
Yes	19 (19.0)	15 (17.0)	65 (63.0)	100	(33.9)
No	79 (81.0)	74 (81.0)	39 (38.0)	193	(65.4)
In AA now?					
Yes	20 (20.0)	8 (9.0)	73 (70.0)	101	(34.2)
No	78 (80.0)	83 (91.0)	31 (30.0)	194	(65.8)
In AA in the past?					
Yes	57 (58.0)	55 (60.0)	93 (89.0)	206	(69.8)
No	38 (39.0)	31 (34.0)	10 (10.0)	80	(31.0)
Abstinent?					
Yes	45 (46.0)	46 (51.0)	90 (87.0)	187	(61.7)
No	52 (53.0)	44 (48.0)	14 (14.0)	111	(37.6)

they had 'some college' (9.5 percent), 39 had bachelor degrees (13.2 percent), 218 had graduate degrees (73.9 percent), six had medical degrees (2 percent), and three indicated they had 'other' educational backgrounds (1.0 percent). Eighty-one providers indicated they were Protestants (27.5 percent), 46 were Catholic (15.6 percent), 42 were Jewish (14.2 percent), 22 were atheist (7.5 percent), 30 were agnostic (10.2 percent), and 64 indicated 'other' regarding religious background (21.7 percent). One hundred fifty three people indicated they were certified as treatment providers (51.9 percent) and 142 indicated they were not (48.1).

Treatment-Provider Groups

Treatment-provider groups included 98 (33.2 percent) from SPAB, 63 (64 percent) males and 35 (36 percent) females; 91 (30.8 percent) from RRS, 69 (76 percent) males and 22 (24 percent) females; and 104 (35.3 percent) from NAADAC, 53 (51 percent) males and 51 (49 percent) females. The three groups varied significantly by sex: there were significant differences in the number of providers who were male and female among the three groups.

Treatment providers were also asked to state what percentage of addicts they believed could recover from their addiction without treatment. They were asked to mark a percentage score from zero to 100.

Results of the Study

Addiction-treatment providers believe, on average, that about 25 percent of addicts recover without treatment. The beliefs of treatment providers about the meaning of addiction are negatively correlated with scores on the ABS. The correlation is statistically significant. What this means is that the stronger the addiction-treatment providers believe addicts can recover without treatment, the stronger is their belief addiction is a choice.

Concurrently, the stronger addiction treatment providers believe addicts cannot recover from addiction without treatment, the stronger their belief in the disease model of addiction. Members of NAADAC scored highest on the ABS (mean = 64.97), followed by those from SPAB (mean = 52.88). Members of RRS scored lowest on the ABS (mean = 42.89). This means that addiction-treatment providers who belong to the NAADAC believe most strongly in the disease-model of addiction, followed by those who are (now) members of Division 50 of the American Psychological Asociation, and then by those in Rational Recovery.

Being a woman is positively associated with ABS score. The mean score on the ABS for females equaled 59.60 and for males 50.91. This means that females tend to believe in the disease model. Males tend to believe in the free-will model. That difference is statistically significant, that is, it's beyond that expected by chance.

Being in AA now is positively associated with ABS scores. The mean score on the ABS for those in AA now was 64.43 and for those not in AA now 48.75. This means that addiction-treatment providers who are in AA now tend to believe in the disease model. Those who are not in AA now tend to believe in the free-will model.

Being certified as an addiction-treatment provider is positively associated with ABS score. The mean score on the ABS for those certified was 57.44 and for those not certified 50.54. This means addiction-treatment providers who are certified tend to believe in

Table 5. Mean Scores for the Spiritual Belief Scale (SBS)a

	Mean	SD	n	p
SBS	24.27	8.55	294	
Gender				.002
Males	23.11	8.84	185	
Females	26.24	7.67	109	
Professional Group				<.001
SPAB	23.93	7.07	97	
RRS	17.75	7.23	91	
NAADAC	30.37	6.32	104	
Religious affiliation				<.001
Catholic	29.02	6.83	46	
Protestant	28.91	6.63	81	
Jewish	21.93	6.34	42	
Agnostic	17.60	4.99	30	
Atheist	11.27	2.62	22	
Other	24.64	8.49	64	
Certified?				.007
Yes	25.55	8.81	153	
No	22.89	8.05	14	
In recovery?				<.001
Yes	28.70	7.21	100	
No	22.04	8.31	192	
In AA now?				<.001
Yes	30.48	5.82	101	
No	21.03	7.94	193	
In AA in the past?				<.001
Yes	26.15	8.33	206	
No	19.25	7.01	79	
Abstinent?				<.001
Yes	26.49	8.42	181	
No	20.65	7.55	111	

Note. The highest possible score is 40. The higher the score, the stronger the spiritual thinking.

the disease model. Those who are not certified tend to believe addiction is a choice, that is, in the free-will model. Certification entails being steeped in the idea that addiction is a disease, not a choice.

The mean score on the SBS was 24.27. Statistically-significant differences in scores on the SBS by gender, certification status, addict-in-recovery status, AA status, abstinence status, and treatment-provider group membership are presented in Table 4. What this means is the differences in average scores on the SBS was beyond that expected by chance.

8

Busting the
Disease-Model Cult

We sincerely addict ourselves to Almighty God.

Thomas Fuller (1655)

Members of a cult behave like a colony of insects when disturbed. A challenge to the cult's beliefs stirs up a frenzy of activity, directed toward protecting the beliefs and attacking the outsider who has challenged them.

Although Alcoholics Anonymous is a religious cult, I am here looking at the broader cult of those who, in the teeth of all fact and reason, preach the disease model. The great majority of these have at least some past involvement with AA. I do not define someone as a cult member just because they accept the disease model: I am looking at those many disease model advocates, inside and outside AA, who behave cultishly.

The AA Cult

It has been widely recognized by social scientists that AA itself is a classic cult, and I will mention only a handfull of sources here.

Sociologists Greil and Rudy looked at the process of conversion to the AA world-view, and concluded that involvement with AA is more likely to involve a high degree of coercion than other cases of religious conversion (1983, p. 23). The central dynamic in the AA conversion process is being brought to accept the opinions of AA, not just about drinking but about life in general. The process of individual recruitment to AA "entails a radical transformation of personal identity," in that the AA message "provides the prospective affiliate not merely with a solution to problems related to drinking, but also with an overarching world view with which the convert can and must reinterpret his or her past experience" (p. 6).

Alexander and Rollins describe how the eight brainwashing techniques employed by the Chinese Communists, identified by Lifton, operate in AA. According to Alexander and Rollins, "AA uses all the methods of brain washing, which are also the methods employed by cults" (Alexander and Rollins 1984, p. 45).

Galanter compares AA with the Unification Church:

> As in the Unification Church workshops, most of those attending AA chapter meetings are deeply involved in the group ethos, and the expression of views opposed to the group's model of treatment is subtly or expressly discouraged. A good example is the fellowship's response to the concept of controlled drinking, an approach to alcoholism treatment based on limiting alcohol intake rather than totally abstaining. Some investigators and clinicians have reported success with this alternative to treatment. The approach, however, is unacceptable within the AA tradition, and the option is therefore anathema to active members. It is rarely brought up by speakers at meetings and suppressed when it is raised. As an inductee becomes involved in the group, the sponsor monitors the person's views carefully, assuring that the recruit adheres to the perspective into which the sponsor was drawn; any hint of an interest in controlled drinking is discouraged. Similar constraints would be applied if a recruit questioned the importance of any of the Steps or the need to attend meetings regularly. . . . As a charismatic group, AA is able to suppress attitudes that could undermine its traditions. (Galanter 1989, p. 185)

Many heavy drinkers with a recognized 'drinking problem' have graduated to moderate or occasional recreational or social drinking. The same applies to many users of other drugs, such as cocaine. AA teaches that the only way for an alcoholic to recover is total abstinence, a demonstrably false assertion accepted on faith. It can be made to seem even remotely plausible only by claiming that all heavy drinkers who moderate thereby show they were never 'alcoholics'. It's easy to surmise why a religious group like AA would adopt such a position: 'controlled drinking' draws attention to the fact that the drinker is in control, that the drinker always has a choice. The cornerstone of AA doctrine is the total helplessness and lack of choice of the alcoholic.

Sadler points out that "AAers seek a relationship with the supernatural in order to cease managing their own lives." AA tells the new recruit that

> his life is unmanageable and that it is ridiculous for him to try to manage it. . . By deliberately denying the ability to control their lives, AAers' former drunken situations are brought under control . . . Most importantly, abstinence is not considered a kind of control. The individual who comes to AA in order to control his drinking will be disappointed. AAers insist that abstinence is possible only when powerlessness is conceded. AA offers supportive interaction in which powerlessness comes to be positively valued. (Sadler 1977, p. 208)

Cult Dogma versus Logic

The most upsetting challenge to the disease model cultist is the claim that addiction is a choice. Not only is this claim supported by science, it has traditionally been viewed as common sense. Here we see a disease model evangelist, in the guise of a psychotherapist, giving her own account of how to stamp out common sense in one of her client's families, or as she puts it, to "counter resistance to acceptance of the disease concept in alcoholic families":

COUNSELOR: We are dealing here with an illness. We know it is an illness because it is predictable (it follows a course which we can describe in advance), it is progressive (it gets worse unless it can be brought into remission), and, if untreated, alcoholism is 100 percent fatal.

FAMILY: All he has to do to straighten up is to want to do it. He just doesn't want to stop drinking. I don't buy that he has a disease.

COUNSELOR: So you see him as just weak-willed. And when he chooses the bottle instead of his family, you feel he doesn't care about you.

FAMILY: Yeah, that's right. He'll step all over you. He makes promises he doesn't keep, and I don't believe he means to keep them when he makes them.

COUNSELOR: Have you ever had diarrhea?

FAMILY: (Laughing a little and looking at the counselor rather strangely) Of course.

COUNSELOR: Did you ever try to control it with willpower?

FAMILY: No. I mean . . . you can't (still chuckling).

COUNSELOR: Why not?

FAMILY: Well, its a bacteria or something. There's nothing you can do about it. . . . Oh . . .

COUNSELOR: You have the idea. Your Dad has an illness he can't fix with willpower because that doesn't stop it. There are things you can do to get diarrhea to stop, just as there are things you can do to stop the active part of alcoholism. But all you can do for both is to set up the conditions under which getting well is possible. It depends on what disease you have. There is a specific treatment for alcoholism . . . (Henderson 1984, pp. 118–19)

Here we see some of the illogical devices of cult persuasion at work. Aside from the blatant untruths that alcoholism always "follows a course which we can describe in advance," always "gets worse" unless "brought into remission," and is always fatal "if untreated" (implying the further falsehood that "treatment" for "alcoholism" is effective), it does not at all follow that something is an illness simply because it is predictable, nor because it is progressive, nor because it is fatal if untreated. Not wanting to stop drinking is a sign of an iron will, not a weak will. The counselor contradicts herself by saying both that the client doesn't have a choice regarding his drinking and that the client chooses the bottle over his family.

Diarrhea is a physical sign of a physical illness. Drinking is purposeful behavior. If you have diarrhea, you are not then required to perform a co-ordinated series of conscious and deliberate goal-directed actions to keep the diarrhea going, whereas this is precisely what you have to do to keep on drinking alcoholic beverages. This psychotherapist is unwilling to acknowledge the dramatic difference between diarrhea and drinking. A sacred dogma is substituted for the recognition of mundane reality, and the preaching of this dogma masquerades as treatment for the family's alleged 'psycho-pathology', a projection of the therapist's.

How the Cult Maintains Its Grip

Cults serve diverse purposes for individuals. These purposes include providing a positive sense of community where values are focused, affirmed, and reinforced. The relationship among individuals in a cult is also hypnotic (Freud 1959; Becker 1973). Individuals who disagree with an ideology binding individuals together in a group are likely to be criticized, punished, and eventually excluded or shunned by the group. The first rule of the cult is 'Thou shalt not disagree'. Affiliation and membership in the cult rests on the establishment and maintenance of an ideological consensus. For the cult to maintain its singular identity, the rule must be obeyed. Break the rule and you break the spell. In order for a singular group identity to persist, individual identities must be contained.

The flip-side of this phenomenon concerns the impact of individual autonomy on the cult experience—a kind of 'psychological capitalism' in a psychologically socialist world. The stronger an individual's confidence in self, the less likely an individual will succumb to demands for cult conformity.

At least three dimensions to those ideas are worth considering: (a) Individuals with a strong sense of personal autonomy are less likely to become involved in cults. (b) If they do become involved in a cult, they are more likely to recover from the cult experience in a way that preserves a strong sense of self (compared to those whose self-concept was considerably weaker prior to the cult experience). (c) What's also likely to be true is that individuals with a strong sense of self are less likely to feel threatened when cult members attack them.

Individuals eschewing cult affiliation may elicit resentment from true believers (Kaufmann 1973). However, some members are split in their involvement with the cult. They may value the ideology and not the affiliation, or vice versa. In the former case they hold fast to the ideology, yet do not attend cult functions. In the latter case they hold fast to the affiliation and seem to know little about the ideology, nor do they seem to care to.

Individuals with backgrounds involving chronic identity confusion, excessive guilt, and 'totalistic' or dichotomous thinking appear to experience more difficulty in re-establishing themselves in their post-cult life, compared to those individuals with a clearer sense of identity, less guilt, and an accurate psychological perspective on themselves and others (Lifton 1961).

In clinical hypnosis, the will of the subject becomes confluent with the will of the hypnotist. The sense of ego separateness between the two is purposely obscured by the hypnotist. In psychotherapy this experience is sometimes called 'transference'. As long as people in either hypnosis or psychotherapy utilizing the concept of transference maintain an acute awareness of self, that is, they persist in appreciating the difference between self and environment, a point referred to as the 'ego boundary' by Fritz Perls (1969), the hypnosis will fail. Some schools of psychotherapy may view this as an obstruction to good therapy while others view it as a means to achieving success (Szasz 1965).

Good contact and a hypnotic trance are opposing states of consciousness. Good contact is an antidote to the cult's hypnotic spell. Moreover, good contact between therapist and client is not contingent upon cultivating transference. Therapy fails when the client chooses to see the therapist as someone other than he or she really is and when therapists encourage clients to see them as someone other than who they really are.

A fictional example of this ability to resist hypnosis (sometimes referred to as brainwashing) is seen in the movie *The Ipcress File* (1965). By deliberately pressing a metal nail into his hand, Harry Palmer (Michael Caine) used his experience of pain to force an awareness of self. He avoided listening to the hypnotic voice of an 'other' seeking to make Palmer's will confluent with his own—against Palmer's will. Palmer found a way to maintain autonomy in the face of psychological coercion. He was able to fight the psychological influence of an other intent on dictating a particular self-concept. By focusing on himself in such a way, he successfully resisted the attempt by the other to force a psychological merge.

How the Cult Attacks Its Critics

For many years now I have been involved in investigating claims made by politicians, drug users, people in 'recovery', members of the addiction-treatment industry, and scholars in the addiction-research field regarding the disease model of addiction, particularly the role of choice in explaining addiction. As we saw in Chapter 3, extensive research supports the theory that addiction is a choice, a behavior better explained by psychological and environmental factors than by physiology and the chemical properties of drugs.

Presenting those findings to people holding opposing points of view, that is, to those who believe addiction is a disease characterized by 'loss of control', often elicits a vituperative response. That response aroused my curiosity as to the cult-like nature of groups within the addiction field.

I've had many encounters with disease-model proponents over the years and I will not elaborate on the details (see Madsen et al. 1990; Goodwin and Gordis 1988). Those exchanges occurred on the editorial pages of large and small newspapers, live radio-talk shows, scientific journals, local political settings, and on some of the first newsgroups on the Internet concerned with addiction. *Ad hominem* rebuttals are standard (Fingarette 1989; Peele 1992; Searles 1993; Madsen 1989; Wallace 1993a; 1993b).

When ideas regarding choice, responsibility, and addiction are introduced to true believers in the disease concept of addiction, the following responses (in no particular order) are likely to occur:

Name-Calling

The person introducing the taboo ideas (whom I refer to as the heretic) is belittled and mocked. Derogatory comments are leveled. Name calling often ensues, for example, I have been called a "thoughtless dweeb," and a "crackpot psychologist," "fascist," "doctor baby," an "arrogant son of a bitch," "contemptible," "immature for a guy with a Dr. before his name," and a person engaging in "highly unscientific behavior," who has embarked on a "personal vendetta."

Accusations of Murder

After the initial mocking and belittling, the hostile response takes a more serious turn. The ideas presented by the heretic are considered dangerous. People who don't know better will be led astray by the heretic's ideas and kill themselves or others. Therefore the heretic should be held accountable for murder.

The accusation of heretic-as-murderer or potential murderer can be leveled as an unintended result of the ideas presented by the heretic, in which case forgiveness by some cult members is still possible; or it can evolve into rhetoric in which the heretic is described as someone with a deliberate interest in endangering the lives of cult members. The heretic then personifies evil in the minds of cult members. It is at this point the exchange could become physically dangerous.

One particularly irate male, over 2,000 miles away, persistently 'fingered' me on the Internet, a computer process by which the login identity of the news group poster may be ascertained along with a brief biography. Each time it is conducted the person 'fingered' is alerted and his work is interrupted while on-line.

Only In It for the Money

The heretic may also be accused at this point of having an economic investment in his particular point of view. For example, I was accused of trying to pirate potential psychotherapy clients away from AA to make money from them as my psychotherapy clients.

Diagnosis of Mental Illness

Another tack the cult members often take is to accuse the heretic of being mentally ill. The heretical ideas allegedly stem from personal trauma the heretic has not dealt with, and his statements opposing the group ideology are considered 'projections', the function of 'denial', an 'unconscious' process said to be a symptom of his mental illness. The heretic may be accused of expressing an emotional need to receive negative attention in order to feel good about himself.

At this point the heretic may be confronted on a paternalistic basis: 'He's sick. He needs help.' At times, cultists may yield and assume a more compassionate posture in relation to the heretic, trying to convince him he is sick, and that he needs to come to his senses.

It Takes One to Know One

The heretic is often attacked because he is not and never has been a drug addict, and therefore cannot speak on the subject. Frequently the heretic is asked, 'have you ever had a drug problem?' Whereas in the diagnosis of mental illness case the motive driving alleged concern is that the heretic's inappropriate behavior is likely to stem from a mental illness, in this case, if the heretic has not had a drug problem or shared in the problems-of-living experienced by cult members, he is said to be incapable of speaking from legitimate experience. It is only by this experience of having been a drug addict that someone can 'know' what the truth is regarding their cult ideology. To the contrary, psychological research on vicarious or observational learning shows that people do learn from the reported and observed experience of others.

There's irony in the fact that many disease-model believers utilize both defensive ploys: the critic is mentally ill (and therefore what he says should be discounted) and the critic is not a recovered addict (and therefore what he says should be discounted). The great majority of disease-model believers in the addiction field are themselves recovered addicts, which accounts for their interest in addiction. They accept the AA doctrine that an addict can never be 'cured', because the addict has a hereditary mental illness, but can only yield to the 'higher power' and totally abstain thereafter. The addict is predetermined to remain an addict 'in remission' even unto death. Thus, disease-model believers hold simultaneously that they themselves are mentally ill, and therefore know what they're talking about, and that their critics are mentally ill, and therefore don't know what they're talking about.

Invoking Authority

A demand for scientific evidence supporting the heretical ideas always emerges. In AA, members often cite scientific findings, usually misleadingly, to support their claims regarding their assertion that addiction is not a choice. The fact that certain medical organizations have endorsed their ideology is brought forth as evidence of the factual basis of their ideas. When scientific evidence to the contrary is presented by the heretic, the research is said to be too old to be valid, not extensive enough, subject to diverse interpretations, and ultimately no match for personal experience. At times, when scientific information is brought into the discussion by the heretic, other scientists will accuse the heretic of unethical use of knowledge and influence, and threaten to report him to some professional association with hopes he will be censured.

When the demand for scientific evidence is met by the heretic, a retreat to 'It takes one to know one' may occur. One person wrote recently: "You sight [sic] science. I sight experience, strength, hope." A favorite evasive ploy is 'Don't criticize what is unless you can propose a better way.' Others are 'Your sources are not scientific enough,' and 'Your understanding of science is not sophisticated enough.'

Shaming

The assault on the heretic is based on the idea that to insist on the cold facts is cruel and insensitive to people who have done him no harm. 'Is this the way you treat your friends or patients?'

Recognizing a Cult and Busting It

The simplest way to test whether a group of people who think alike is a cult is to see how they respond to disagreement with their core beliefs. Most cults tolerate disagreement over peripheral issues, but come down furiously on any dissent from the core principles. Cults usually follow practices, such as the "thought-terminating cliché" (Lifton 1961) to close off certain dangerous lines of discussion. Often, members will be scorned, or worse, for reading dangerous books or having contacts with dangerous individuals. The stronger the evidence against the cult's core beliefs, the more emotional and inflexible the response to presentation of that evidence. The worst cults discourage social interaction between members and outsiders.

The Internet is an opportunity for cults, but even more of a threat to their survival. Devices like the 'kill file' will be employed by cults faced with Internet criticism. A kill file automatically prevents their computers from displaying anything by a listed person (the heretic) on the screen.

The critic should boldly challenge the cult, without trying to disguise or minimize the areas of disagreement. If the cult is unused to critical challenges, some members will defect from it quite quickly. Others will be prepared to engage in a dialogue with the heretic, which may eventually break the cult's hypnotic spell.

Humor is useful to reduce the tension in confrontations, and for this reason many cults will place a ban on humor in 'serious' contexts—areas related to the core beliefs. Attempts to break off all contact between cult members and the heretic are a sign that the heretic's criticisms are hitting home. Since cult members will always tend to conceal internal dissension or doubts from outsiders, critics should be confident that whatever they say is having more long-term impact than is apparent on the surface.

9

The Project MATCH
Cover-Up

> These contradictions are not accidental, nor do they
> result from ordinary hypocrisy: they are deliberate
> exercises in doublethink. For it is only by reconciling
> contradictions that power can be retained indefinitely.
>
> George Orwell, *Nineteen Eighty-Four*

The Project MATCH affair is a case study in the duplicity of the
Therapeutic State. About $35 million of the taxpayers' money was
spent on a mammoth study of alcoholism treatment. The findings
were the opposite of what the organizers of the study wanted.

The study showed that no type of treatment for alcoholism is
significantly better or worse than any other, and in particular, that
'treatment' by free self-help groups is at least as good as 'treatment'
by paid professionals. Every effort was then made to suppress
these findings and to smear those who publicized them.

The Scope of Project MATCH

MATCH stands for 'Matching Alcoholism Treatment to Client
Heterogeneity'. Here's a description of Project MATCH in 1995,
when it was under way but the results were not yet in, by Dr. Enoch

95

Gordis, director of the National Institute on Alcohol Abuse and Alcoholism (NIAAA):

> This study is the first national, multisite trial of patient-treatment matching and one of the two largest current initiatives of NIAAA. Established under a cooperative agreement that allows direct collaboration between the Institute and the researcher, the project involves nine geographically representative clinical sites and a data coordinating center. Researchers in Project MATCH are among the most senior and experienced treatment scientists in the field. Both public and private treatment facilities, as well as hospital and university outpatient facilities, are represented. (Gordis 1995, vii)

The impetus for this ambitious project appears to have been, in part, the National Academy of Sciences Institute of Medicine report entitled *Broadening the Base of Treatment for Alcohol Problems* (1990), which characterizes heavy drinkers as a heterogeneous population. Hypothetically, said the authors, a single-treatment approach, for example, Alcoholics Anonymous-based treatment, to helping heavy drinkers is not therapeutic for everyone (see Donovan and Mattson 1994). Since drinkers vary, treatment should vary.

A mean-spirited cynic might unpack this suggestion in the following way: AA gets a lot of respect, and is the source of many of the ideas in alcoholism treatment. But if AA works, it becomes difficult to justify costly treatment by paid professionals. How can we both justify the rapidly expanding addiction treatment industry, with its numerous employment opportunities for addiction experts like ourselves, and avoid knocking AA? Answer: both professional treatment and AA are effective, but for different kinds of alcoholics.

Matching treatment protocol to the heterogeneous nature of the heavy-drinker population makes sense, once we accept the basic premises of alcoholism treatment. For what it's worth, I absolutely agree that 'alcoholics' are a heterogeneous population, and too much discussion assumes they are all alike.

Project MATCH tried to determine whether three treatment approaches varied in effectiveness when clients were matched accordingly (treatment deemed most appropriate). The three independent variables were TSF (twelve-step facilitation therapy; see Nowinski, Baker, and Carroll 1995), CBT (cognitive-behavioral coping skills therapy; see Kadden et al. 1995), and MET (motivational enhancement therapy; see Miller et al. 1995). "Because the three treatments can be readily taught and incorporated into a variety of treatment settings, the study could have a major impact on delivery of treatment services" (Project MATCH Research Group 1993, p. 1142). The generalizability of findings appeared strong. The dependent measures included percentage levels of abstinence and drinks per day.

Findings of Project MATCH

On June 25, 1996, I attended a symposium entitled 'Project MATCH: Treatment: Main Effects and Matching Results'. That public presentation was sponsored by the 1996 Joint Scientific Meeting of the Research Society on Alcoholism (RSA) and the International Society for Biomedical Research on Alcoholism in Washington, D.C. At the symposium, the Project MATCH Research Group presented its findings, which included the following:

1. There were excellent overall outcomes, which means that a substantial number of subjects became abstinent or reduced their daily consumption of beverage alcohol.
2. There were few differences in the effectiveness of the three treatment approaches, and any differences were not statistically significant. Those assigned to TSF did slightly better than those assigned to the CBT group. The MET group did the least well. Again, those differences were attributable to chance only.
3. Matching clients to particular treatments has no effect. Mismatches are not a major obstacle.
4. TSF is associated with better outcomes (based on the dependent measures used). But, again, the difference is so small as to be attributable to chance only.

Let's just consider what these findings mean. Finding 1. would be remarkable if it were true, but although this was claimed as a finding, Project MATCH was unable to support it with solid evidence, for a very simple reason: there was no control group of alcoholics who received no treatment. A substantial number of untreated alcoholics will, over a period of time, either become abstinent or reduce their daily consumption. The question is whether a similar population of alcoholics will yield a *bigger* 'substantial number' if treatment is given. There is no reason to suppose that this is true. In fact, if a number of different treatments, dramatically at odds in their assumptions and techniques, achieve the same results, it seems reasonable to conjecture that the zero option, no treatment, will also achieve the same results.

The most interesting and embarrassing finding is number 2. TSF (Twelve Step Facilitation, the AA approach) did better than the others, but the difference was so slight that it was probably due to chance. Just consider the implications of this. TSF, CBT, and MET are very, very different, but they all achieve the same degree of 'success'. The treatment approach associated with a religiously-motivated self-help group does just as 'well' as treatment approaches associated with skilled professional counselors. The implication is clear: alcoholism treatment facilities don't provide any return for the money 'invested' in them.

Furthermore, the Project drew a blank on the very issue it was specifically trying to test, and perhaps hoping to verify. Nothing is to be gained by 'matching' different types of heavy drinkers with different types of 'treatments'.

In view of what was to come, we need to ask at this point: were these really the findings of Project MATCH? They certainly were the findings reported to the symposium by Project MATCH researchers and noted down by me. I reported those findings on several Internet mail lists at St. John's University in Jamaica, N.Y., and discussion ensued. The accuracy of my report was confirmed (at my public suggestion) by Alex Taylor, a former student of mine who had become a reporter for the Drug Policy Foundation (DPF) in Washington, D.C. Taylor wrote a brief story on the MATCH report for the *Drug Policy Letter* (News item, 1996). He telephoned Margaret E. Mattson, Project MATCH staff collaborator and monograph series editor, Division of Clinical and Prevention Research at NIAAA. She consented to have her conversation with him tape-recorded for his story. Taylor read my report of findings to Dr. Mattson and she confirmed them as accurate on June 28th, 1996.

It seems clear enough, then, that these were indeed the findings of Project MATCH, and that they were endorsed as such, without qualification, by Dr. Mattson. But between 28th June and 19th July, something remarkable must have happened.

Denial!

On July 19th, Dr. Mattson posted on the Internet a letter sent to me via certified mail from Dr. Ronald Kadden, chair of the Project MATCH Steering Committee. It appeared, before I had seen it, on addict-l@listserv.kent.edu (a public Internet mail list described as "Academic and Scholarly discussion of addiction related topics"). She also posted a private letter I had not yet received in the mail on a public list of which I am not a member. Dr. Gerard Connors, a principal investigator with the Project MATCH Research Group at the Research Institute on Addictions, Buffalo, did a similar thing. He posted the letter on a recovery-based, controlled-drinking mail list (mm@sjuvm.stjohns.edu), one I had created. They each prefaced the posted letter with the following statement: "Ron Kadden, in his capacity as Chair of the Project MATCH Research Group, has asked me to post this message. The actual letter has been mailed to Dr. Schaler." Here is the first part of the letter:

> Dear Dr. Schaler:
>
> It has come to the attention of the Project MATCH Research Group that there has been considerable discussion on the Internet regarding the results of the trial. Unfortunately, several of the communications that we have been shown contain a number of inaccuracies and thus do not adequately represent the trial nor its results as presented at RSA. Further, none of the results or interpretations that are being circulated have been confirmed by Dr. Margaret Mattson or anyone else in the Project MATCH Research Group, despite assertions they were.

I forwarded a copy of the posted letter to Alex Taylor, as he had informed me that Mattson had confirmed my report of the findings as accurate. Taylor immediately telephoned Mattson, Gordis, Kadden, and Anne Bradley (the press secretary for NIAAA), to discuss Kadden's public assertion that "none of the results or interpretations that are being circulated have been confirmed by Dr. Margaret Mattson or anyone else in the Project MATCH Research Group." Mattson, Gordis, and Kadden did not return Taylor's calls. Dr. Thomas F. Babor (another principal investigator of the MATCH project) and Ms. Bradley returned Taylor's call. (Taylor had not called Babor.) Babor refused to have his conversation with Taylor taped. Babor *confirmed my report of the findings to Taylor as accurate* but claimed that an inference I had drawn was incorrect: the

TSF variable, he contended, was different from AA-based treatment, that is, he asserted that the MATCH study had not tested the effectiveness of AA-style treatment.

NIAAA Press Secretary Anne Bradley consented to having her conversation with Taylor taped. He informed her that Mattson's confirmation was taped with consent. Bradley stated in her official capacity (on tape with her consent) that Mattson had confirmed my report of the MATCH findings as accurate. NIAAA thereby contradicted Drs. Mattson and Kadden and the Project MATCH Research Group. Apparently, Drs. Mattson, Connors, and Kadden, in their official capacities as members and representatives of the Project MATCH Research Group, were not being entirely forthright. They used their taxpayer-funded professional positions to publicly announce that my statements were inaccurate when in fact my statements were perfectly accurate.

Is TSF the AA's Approach?

Dr. Kadden's letter to me continued:

> Some of the inaccuracies involve the treatments. For example, the Twelve Step Facilitation treatment is NOT a test of Alcoholics Anonymous. It would be useful for interested parties to refer to the treatment manuals, which are available from the National Clearinghouse for Alcohol and Drug Information.

You will remember that Aristotle, the founder of logic, started from the proposition that a thing is itself: A is A. But if A is A, can AA sometimes not be AA? Apparently, AA ceases to be AA when psychologists working for the government call it TSF. Is there anything in Kadden's suggestion that TSF and AA are different? Here is Project MATCH's own account of why the TSF variable was chosen:

> The Twelve-Step approach of AA was selected because of widespread belief in the effectiveness of this approach. . . . Given the widespread popularity of the AA Twelve-Step approach, any matching effects found for it would be highly transportable. (Project MATCH Research Group 1993, p. 1132)

Presumably "highly transportable" means that the effects of this particular example of an AA Twelve-Step approach could be generalized to other examples. And what about the TSF manual that

Kadden had suggested "interested parties" ought to refer to? Here's what it says:

> Twelve Step Facilitation Approach. This therapy is grounded in the concept of alcoholism as a spiritual and medical disease. The content of this intervention is consistent with the 12 Steps of Alcoholics Anonymous (AA), with primary emphasis given to Steps 1 through 5. In addition to abstinence from alcohol, a major goal of the treatment is to foster the patient's commitment to participation in AA. During the course of the program's 12 sessions, patients are actively encouraged to attend AA meetings and to maintain journals of their AA attendance and participation. Therapy sessions are highly structured, following a similar format each week that includes symptoms inquiry, review and reinforcement for AA participation, introduction and explication of the week's theme, and setting goals for AA participation for the next week. Material introduced during treatment sessions is complemented by reading assignments from AA literature. (Nowinski et al. 1995, p. x)

> The therapeutic approach underlying this manual is grounded in the principles and 12 Steps of AA. (p. xi)

> The program described here is intended to be consistent with active involvement in Alcoholics Anonymous. . . . It adheres to the concepts set forth in the 'Twelve Steps and Twelve Traditions' of Alcoholics Anonymous. . . . The overall goal of this program is to facilitate patients' active participation in the fellowship of AA. It regards such active involvement as the primary factor responsible for sustained sobriety ('recovery') and therefore as the desired outcome of participation in this program. (p. 1)

> The two major treatment goals are reflected in a series of specific objectives that are congruent with the AA view of alcoholism. (p. 3)

> Central to this approach is strong encouragement of the patient to attend several AA meetings per week of different kinds and to read the 'Big Book' ('Alcoholics Anonymous') as well as other AA publications throughout the course of treatment. (p. 4)

> The goal of the conjoint sessions is to educate the partner regarding alcoholism and the AA model, to introduce the concept of enabling, and to encourage partners to make a commitment to attend six Al-Anon meetings of their choice. (p. 5)

> Suggestions made by the 12-Step therapist should be consistent with what is found in AA-approved publications such as those that are recommended to patients. (p. 8)

Encouraging patients to actively work the 12 Steps of Alcoholics Anonymous is the primary goal of treatment, as opposed to any skill that the therapist can teach. (p. 10)

The therapist acts as a resource and advocate of the 12-Step approach to recovery (p. 11)

In this program, the fellowship of AA, and not the individual therapist, is seen as the major agent of change (p. 14)

There is . . . no cure for alcoholism; rather, there is only a method for arresting the process, which is active participation in the 12-Step program of Alcoholics Anonymous. (p. 33).

Why would Drs. Babor and Kadden and the Project MATCH Research Group try to obscure the fact that TSF is essentially the same as AA, when their own literature says as much? Would they have denied this if the Project MATCH findings had been different, for example, if a statistically significant difference in treatment effects had been found?

Spin Doctoring by Project MATCH

Dr. Kadden concluded his letter to me with the following:

We recognize that there is some impatience in the field to draw inferences from our findings. However, we believe that this can only be done in a scientifically valid way once the entire field has access to the findings. We therefore respectfully request that you and others wait for the paper that is to be published in the *Journal of Studies on Alcohol* in Jan. 1997 before drawing any conclusions, or implications regarding policy issues. Thank you for your consideration of this request.

For the Project MATCH Research Group,
Ronald Kadden, Ph.D.
Chairman, Project MATCH Steering Committee

Whose impatience? How do they "recognize" this impatience? There had been no clamor to hear the findings before they volunteered them to the Washington, D.C., conference. The "paper" mentioned by Dr. Kadden did later appear, and completely confirmed my account (Project MATCH Research Group 1997a). Given the tardy way in which such articles move from completion to publication, Dr. Kadden must have known this was so when he wrote the above letter.

Remember, the Project MATCH Research Group (employee) works for the American taxpayer (employer). We are confronted with a situation here in which a group of employees tell a select group called 'scientists' about the results of their publicly funded project. Then, the employer is told by the employees not to talk about the findings, that is, the employees dictate employer behavior!

Dr. Stanton Peele wrote this to me about the Project MATCH Research Group's shameless attempts at spin doctoring:

> The MATCH researchers and NIAAA administrators have insisted that interested professionals not discuss the results they announced at an open conference until they can spin them in their uncontested presentations and articles. They are acting like the military officials who embargoed their reports on missile hits during the Gulf War (and perhaps with the same aim of covering up exaggerated claims of success). But isn't a research organization, unlike a military one, supposed to encourage open discussion of ideas and data? Not, apparently, when the principals are nervous about spending multimillions while failing to support the patient-treatment matching approach that they have been touting for years! (Personal communication, August 1996; see also Peele 1997)

The Project MATCH Research Groups 'respectful request' is a euphemism for state-sanctioned restrictions on freedom of speech. NIAAA tried to pressure the Drug Policy Foundation into not publishing the news item by Alex Taylor. One reason for doing so is suggested above by Stanton Peele: The results of the $35 million project fail "to support the patient-treatment matching approach that they have been touting for years." In other words, according to the researchers' findings, it makes no difference whether heavy drinkers are treated as a homogeneous or as a heterogeneous population.

They didn't get the results they were hoping for, so they began to backpedal. They tried to implement damage control by making the unsupported claim that treatment works.

Selling Water by the River

What might the Project MATCH Research Group's motivation for cover-up be? Note there was no statistically significant difference among cognitive-behavioral coping skills, motivational enhancement therapy, and twelve-step facilitation therapy in terms of achieving abstinence or reducing drinking. CBT and MET are generally part of professional-treatment programs. TSF is based in a self-help program, that is, AA.

The reasonable answer to the question posed is this: the Project MATCH Research Group is afraid that its findings will support the abolition of professional treatment for heavy drinking, and concomittantly for addiction in general. There's no reason to pay for professional treatment when free self-help programs such as AA (or free self-help programs based on CBT or MET) are equally effective. Paying for treatment when a consumer can get it free simply doesn't make sense.

So-called 'scientifically proven effective' approaches to helping heavy drinkers such as CBT and MET appear to be no more effective than the essence of one based on religion. Whether the clients are matched or not matched to the most appropriate treatment, the effectiveness is the same insofar as achieving abstinence or reducing the number of drinks consumed.

Health-management organizations, insurance companies, and Congress should consider that interpretation carefully. Why should taxpayers support ever-expanding but evidently ineffective treatment for heavy drinking or addiction in general? The voluntary self-help movement is growing steadily and continues to meet the diverse needs of heavy drinkers and those generally diagnosed with addiction. In addition to AA there is now SMART Recovery, a secular, cognitive-behavior-therapy approach that's abstinence-oriented. Diverse secular-based controlled-drinking programs are growing in number, too. All these programs are autonomous and free. (I do not recommend another of these groups, Moderation Management. See the next chapter.)

The Project MATCH findings support the idea that selling treatment for heavy drinking alongside free self-help programs such as AA is like selling water by the river, to coin a Zen saying. Why buy when the river gives it for free? Yes, this would likely destroy the economic foundations of the addiction-treatment industry. So what? If the members of that industry sincerely care about heavy drinkers seeking help (as they so often claim to), why wouldn't they welcome the lifting of an economic burden for these people, that is, having to pay for treatment? Whose interests are really being served here?

Dr. Gordis appears to have realized these implications. He began the discussion at the RSA symposium by claiming the Project MATCH findings showed that 'treatment works'. This, he asserted, was because so many people became abstinent or reduced their drinking through all three treatment approaches. At least four members of the audience moved quickly to the microphone and delivered essentially the same rejoinder. I was one of them:

> I would like to reiterate what has just been said. There was no control group. With all due respect, Dr. Gordis, there is no evidence in this study to show that treatment is effective. In fact, there are studies showing no treatment is as effective as treatment.

The studies I was alluding to include Edwards et al. 1977; Chick et al. 1988; and Sobell, Cunningham, and Sobell 1996. If they were widely known and understood, the MATCH study findings could mean the end of the addiction-treatment industry, and be a boon to its competition, the self-help movement. Dr. Gordis tried to avoid this conclusion by attempting to divert discussion to his completely unsubstantiated claim that treatment works.

Why didn't the Project MATCH Research Group challenge Dr. Gordis on that idea? It's clear that AA-type self-help is as effective as cognitive-behavioral coping skills and motivational enhancement therapy. In any case, the whole idea of treatment effectiveness is suspect. Stanton Peele suggested the following study: "Divide the money spent on MATCH by the number of alcoholics MATCH treated, then give this amount to each of a new group of alcoholics and see how much they improve without any professionals in sight" (Personal communication, August 1996).

I agree in essence with this idea: treatment doesn't work, but giving substantial sums of money to addicts as a reward for stopping or moderating their drug intake obviously would work (in the sense that the percentage of addicts stopping or moderating would increase, the bigger the payments the greater the percentage responding appropriately). I don't approve of using taxpayers' money in this way, but if we are going to spend enormous sums to persuade people to stop taking the drugs they now choose to take, why not just bribe the addicts directly, and cut out the middle-man (the addiction treatment industry), who doesn't deliver anyway?

Orwellian Doublethink

Are the organizers of Project MATCH practicing Orwellian double-think? Dr. Margaret Mattson confirmed my report of the MATCH findings as accurate and then posted a letter by the Project MATCH Research Group claiming she had never confirmed them. That's the first contradiction. NIAAA contradicted the assertions in Dr. Kadden's letter. That's the second contradiction. The claim by Drs. Kadden and Babor that twelve-step facilitation therapy and AA are substantively different from one another is contradicted by the official manuals they recommend. That's the third contradiction. On the one hand, the Project MATCH Research Group findings were presented at an open symposium. On the other hand, it asks that those findings not be discussed. That's the fourth contradiction. Dr. Gordis asserted that the MATCH study findings show 'treatment works'. Yet no control group was used for comparison. That's the fifth contradiction.

To repeat Orwell's words, these contradictions expressed by NIAAA and the Project MATCH Research Group "are not accidental, nor do they result from ordinary hypocrisy: they are deliberate exercises in doublethink." They are acts of aggression not directed toward any one individual but toward individualism and autonomy (in the form of self-help groups such as AA, for example) as general forces threatening the authority of the state. They are directed against anyone who dares to oppose the sanctity of the Therapeutic State and the economic interests of the growing treatment industry.

10

Moderation Management and Murder

The man who is . . . addicted and destined to death.

Philemon Holland, *Livy's Roman History* (1600)

In about 1993 I received a call from Audrey Kishline who was thinking of founding a new self-help group to promote moderate drinking rather than total abstinence. Ms. Kishline had been referred to me by Herbert Fingarette. She had read his book *Heavy Drinking: The Myth of Alcoholism as a Disease* and was intrigued by his discussion of controlled drinking.

Audrey Kishline had herself had a drinking problem, had been in AA, which she didn't like at all, and then in Rational Recovery, which she also apparently didn't like because of its insistence on abstention. She wanted to start a self-help alternative to Alcoholics Anonymous and Rational Recovery, based on the findings in studies showing that even the heaviest drinkers could moderate their drinking. She asked me for help.

Since I'd been interested for some time in encouraging the growth and development of diverse approaches to helping heavy drinkers and drug users, I agreed to help her. (I have served on the boards of Rational Recovery, SMART Recovery, and Moderation Management.) I helped Ms. Kishline get in touch with leaders in the field of alcohol research such as Stanton Peele, Alan Marlatt, Martha Sanchez-Craig, and Fred Glaser. Audrey Kishline wrote a book entitled *Moderate Drinking: The New Option for Problem Drinkers* (1994), which first appeared with a foreword by me (dropped from recent printings). In addition to helping her with securing the Moderation Management service mark at the U.S Patent Office in Crystal City, Virginia, I was able to get her featured in a film on the disease model of alcoholism produced by James Morrison of U.S. Health Productions, Columbus, Ohio, which aired throughout the U.S. and Canada in 1994–1995, marking the media birth of Moderation Management.

Audrey Kishline, her husband Brian, and I formed the first board of directors of MM. It became incorporated as a non-profit organization in 1995. In Jan 1995 I was interviewed by Leslie Knowlton who was interested in doing a story on MM for the *Los Angeles Times*. The story appeared on January 31st, 1995. A similar story by Knowlton came out in the February 1995 issue of *Psychiatric Times* entitled 'Just One? Exploring Moderation Management.'

Soon thereafter, the producers of NBC's *Leeza* show contacted us. Audrey Kishline and I were flown to Hollywood to tape a show entitled 'Can Alcoholics Drink?' That was taped on March 30th, 1995. It was a raucous show. Audrey Kishline was nervous and the producers of the show had planted the audience with disease-model advocates who were extremely hostile to the idea that heavy drinkers could control their drinking. During the show, to my surprise, Audrey Kishline declared that MM was only for 'problem drinkers', not for people with the disease of alcoholism.

Following that show and largely as a result of it, Audrey Kishline and MM were featured in *The New York Times, Newsweek, Time, Business Week,* and *U.S. News and World Report,* as well as on *The Late, Late Show with Tom Snyder, Good Morning America, ABC World News, Tonight with Peter Jennings, Dateline,* and *Oprah,* among many others.

In 1996 I created an Internet mail list through St. John's University in Jamaica, New York, for people with drinking and drug problems who wanted to use the Moderation Management approach to controlling their consumption. I also created another Internet mail list for the new board of directors we had now gathered together for Moderation Management, Inc.

However, I was becoming uneasy, because Audrey and Brian Kishline continued to emphasize that Moderation Management was appropriate only for 'problem drinkers', not for 'real alcoholics'. They asserted that people with the 'disease of alcoholism' should not attempt moderation, and that they should use an abstinence-oriented approach to their drinking problems. This was in direct contradiction to what I had supposed was the fundamental distinguishing mark of MM.

Critics of Moderation Management began to say that Kishline's program was dangerous for people who had the disease of alcoholism. They asked her how she could tell the difference between 'problem drinkers' and those with the disease of alcoholism. Of course, she could not, since there is no conceivable way to do this: alcoholics just are problem drinkers, end of story. The critics went on to say that those with the disease of alcoholism, understandably wanting to believe they could drink in moderation, were being misled into believing that they could learn to control their drinking when in fact they could not. Loss of control would be triggered because of Moderation Management. This criticism is quite logical, once we accept the premise that there is such a disease as alcoholism for which MM would be inappropriate.

I objected to Audrey and Brian Kishline's view that there was a disease called alcoholism and that somehow people with this putative disease were different from 'problem drinkers'. Since neither they nor anyone else could differentiate between the two, and since the Kishlines believed that some drinkers suffered with the disease of alcoholism, their critics were in effect right to point to the conclusion that MM must be dangerous to alcoholics who were attracted to it. However, I also pointed out that they were misunderstanding the basis upon which MM had apparently been established: MM was founded because of research showing that the heaviest drinkers, that is, precisely those alleged to 'have' the disease of alcoholism, could in fact control their drinking. There has never been any research showing that controlled drinking approaches were appropriate only for non-alcoholic 'problem drinkers', whoever they are.

As more and more publicity of MM became available, the more I emphasized the importance of the false distinction between problem drinkers and those with the disease of alcoholism, as well as the fact that the most important studies on controlled drinking and loss of control had been done with the heaviest drinkers, that is, indisputably those with the strongest claim to have the putative disease called alcoholism.

Brian Kishline told me that I ought to consider resigning from the MM board of directors and I quickly agreed. I severed all relations with MM in 1996.

Getting Away with Murder

On April 30th 1998 I sat down to read the front page of *The New York Times*, and discovered the 'On-line Confession to an Off-line Killing' that had taken place on the Moderation Management Internet list, the list I had created and left to the MM organization a couple of years earlier.

Larry Froistad, a computer programmer in his twenties, a member of the MM list, and a person whose home page on the world wide web (now shut down by the site administrator) indicated significant involvement with MM, had confessed online to murdering his five-year-old daughter.

The *Times* story left the impression that MM listowners Audrey Kishline, founder of MM, and Dr. Frederick Rotgers, Director of the program for Addictions, Consultation, and Treatment at Rutgers University, wanted Larry Froistad to get away with murder.

This episode raises important questions about law and liability for Internet list owners and 'mental health' professionals, to be sure, but it raises serious ethical issues too.

Excerpts from the archives of mm@maelstrom.stjohns.edu were published verbatim in *The New York Times*. Here, in part, is Larry Froistad's confession:

> My God, there's something I haven't mentioned . . . The people I'm mourning the loss of, I've ejected from my life. Kitty had to endure my going to jail twice and being embarrassed in front of her parents. Amanda I murdered because her mother stood between us . . . .
>
> I suffered for years trying to get custody of her after her mother divorced me. When I did, I still had to deal with her mother's constant attempts to take her back. I had the upper hand; in fact, her mother gave up her summer custody just before I killed Amanda. But I always felt I was not in complete control . . . the conflict was tearing me apart, and the next night I let her watch the videos she loved all evening, and when she was asleep I got wickedly drunk, set our house on fire, went

to bed, listened to her scream twice, climbed out the window and set about putting on a show of shock, surprise and grief to remove culpability from myself.

Dammit, part of that show was climbing in her window and grabbing her pajamas, then hearing her breathe and dropping her where she was so she could die and rid me of her mother's interferences. Hearing her wheeze in the smoke which I could barely stand—looking at her bedroom door burning—these are things I can't forget. Those last two screams that I tell everyone saved my life—they are wounds on my soul that I can't heal and that I'm sure I'm meant to carry with me. I am damaged goods, and as much as I feel I need the comfort of someone in my life that I can be good to, someone I can build a new family with—the simple fact is that I don't deserve those things and I'm meant to suffer a thousand times longer than my little girl did.

Here is how Dr. Rotgers responded:

Larry, Several folks have sent me private emails expressing genuine concern over some of the stuff that you've posted very recently. They are concerned, that you might be contemplating suicide or other drastic, harmful and ultimately counterproductive actions aimed at dealing with what seems to have become for you an awful situation. I'm writing for all of the folks who wrote me offlist, and I believe for all of the folks on this list, to urge you to seriously think about contacting a therapist and working things through with yourself in a safe manner. Take care of yourself, my friend. And let us all know how things are going. The people here really care about you.

While any legal obligation to report Froistad's written murder confession to the police is unclear, I maintain that Kishline and Rotgers had an ethical responsibility to report the confession—especially because they led the group. The fact is that they did not report it, but several lay members of the group did. Those who reported Froistad did the right thing, and they deserve to be commended for acting promptly. Instead, they were vilified and ridiculed by members of the MM list and Rotgers himself.

There was an ugly mood of vituperation against those who had squealed on the confessed murderer in their midst. Here's part of an email sent by one chat room member to another who had reported Froistad's confession: "Just how big a pervert are you? I bet you really get off talking to the FBI. Wow. Did you ask them if you could see their guns?"

Why attribute far-fetched motives to those who simply do what is obviously and indisputably right? Why were these members so despised? Ms. Kishline, as reported in *The New York Times* article, said the group "was considering not maintaining archives . . . and issuing a more strongly worded notice to new subscribers that their words . . . can never be considered completely confidential." Why would she want to protect a confessed murderer from exposure? Does Ms. Kishline express any concern for the five-year-old girl who, as far as she knew, quite probably had been murdered? Does she express any concern for the living mother of the dead daughter?

What does Ms. Kishline's statement tell us about her conception of her role in Moderation Management? At first it appears she said this to 'protect the confidentiality' of discussion on the list. However, I suspect that Kishline believes that criminal behavior is 'treatable', that it stems from mental disease, in this case 'addiction disease', and that her self-help group is a more appropriate place to deal with criminal behavior, such as homicide, than the criminal justice system.

Have Nothing to Do with MM

What this episode teaches us is that we should have nothing to do with Moderation Management. Its leaders' warped view of human conduct and grandiose picture of their own role has brought them into a mindset where a confession that a father has murdered his daughter causes them to sympathize with the father and try to prevent the admitted crime from being investigated. Evidently Audrey Kishline placed a higher value on the protocols of her self-help group than on assisting the police with a determination of facts about what could be (and we have subsequently learned, was indeed) a brutal, cold-blooded killing of a child. Ms. Kishline cared little for justice.

Dr. Rotgers's story is slightly different. Based on the statements he made appearing in *The New York Times*, I would have to say that Rotgers, like Kishline, acted unethically. Dr. Rotgers did not notify law-enforcement authorities "since," he is quoted as saying, "the child was already dead"—surely a ghastly slip. Rotgers here tacitly admits that he believed in the accuracy of at least part of Froistad's account. Rotgers believed at least some of what Froistad was saying was true. If the child had died, as he believed was the case, why didn't he act to ensure that the death was investigated?

And even if he had no idea whether the report was true or not, why didn't he act to inform law enforcement, so that we could find out? I believe that the moral obligation to inform the police was not contingent on whether Rotgers could ascertain the truthfulness of Froistad's confession. He had an ethical and a professional responsibility as a psychologist to inform the police so that they—and perhaps a jury—could make that determination. Instead, Rotgers called Froistad "my friend" and encouraged him to see a therapist to 'work things through'.

Rotgers expressed more concern about Froistad's possibly harming himself than about his possibly harming others. Yet if Froistad had murdered his own daugher, why wouldn't he be inclined to harm someone else, perhaps someone less important to him than his own daughter?

The MM confession story appeared on ABC, CBS, and NBC news television two nights in a row following the report in *The New York Times*. People have good reason to be shocked by this story. They are shocked by the heinous nature of the crime. They are shocked by the online written confession. They are shocked by Kishline and Rotgers's failure to report the confession. They are shocked that those who did right by reporting the confession to the police were then attacked by members and leaders in the MM organization.

I understand that some therapists were genuinely embarrassed by this incident, because they had given a general assurance of confidentiality to their clients, and they felt they would be betraying a trust if such an occasion arose in their practice.

I recommend that therapists, counselors, and leaders of self-help groups announce a clear written policy to their clients or members, or to the general public. Details of this policy will vary somewhat among different therapists and groups. But therapists and self-help groups are not defense attorneys, and ought to keep a sense of proportion about the importance of their own role. My practice, which I recommend generally, is to state at the outset that knowledge of any felony *involving direct physical harm to others* will not be protected by the general presumption of confidentiality.

Froistad Convicted

From various news reports, it appears that Froistad made several confessions to the killing, all of which he later retracted. He was indicted for murder, and prepared a defense involving the claim that his mental illness, brought on by grief over the accidental death of his daughter, had made him concoct false confessions. Aside from his confessions, his account of what had actually happened in the burning house—how he had escaped while his daughter had died—had aroused the suspicions of members of the police and the Bowman, North Dakota, fire department.

At first, Froistad's motive for the killing was not clear. But after police seized his computer, they found evidence that Froistad had sexually molested his daughter, that he was heavily involved in child pornography, and that his daughter had made remarks about his behavior to a school employee. Froistad therefore had a clear self-interest in killing his daughter, and only narrowly failed to get away with it, in part because some of the online contributors to the MM internet list had the decency to do what was clearly right, unlike the MM leadership. In October 1998 Froistad was convicted and sentenced to 40 years.

11

Thinking Differently about Addiction

> Persons who addict themselves to vice . . . become
> miserable.
>
> Joseph Priestley (1782)

The idea that addiction is a disease is the greatest medical hoax since the idea that masturbation would make you go blind. This is not to say that the behaviors people now fashionably regard as symptoms of addiction are non-existent. Hundreds of years ago, people exhibiting certain behaviors and minor skin lesions were 'diagnosed' as witches. That didn't and doesn't mean they were actually witches. Anyone is 'diagnosable'. Calling human pursuits diseases tells us more about the diagnostician than it does about the persons being diagnosed.

As psychologist Bruce K. Alexander pointed out years ago, there are good and bad addictions. Good addictions are activities we engage in to enhance our sense of well-being and happiness in life. Pursuing these addictions decreases our experience of suffering. Bad addictions are activities we engage that diminish our sense of well-being and happiness in life. Engaging in these activities increases our experience of suffering.

The Spell of Prozac

A woman turning 45 is unhappy—for many reasons. She needs to make some changes in order to feel more fulfilled in her life. Perhaps she needs to leave her husband. Or change careers. Or work toward a graduate degree. Or get a hobby in order to decrease her feelings of unhappiness, her sense of isolation and her loneliness—her feelings of meaninglessness in life. It doesn't matter right now exactly what changes she needs to make. It could be any of those I've mentioned, or others. She needs to do something in order to make her life more meaningful, and then to feel better.

Yet, for some reason she doesn't take the steps necessary to make those changes. Is it that she cannot take those steps, or is it that she *will not* do so? One might be inclined to say she *will* not do what she needs to do in order to feel better. Others may be inclined to say she cannot do what she needs to do in order to feel better. And still others may be inclined to say that she *cannot will* herself.

Clearly, she's *discouraged*. She seems to lack the courage, for whatever reason, to make those changes. She sits at her desk and stares out the window of her office. Her physician, during a routine check-up, notices her 'affect', that is, her mood, is flat. Still, when her doctor asks her how she feels, she smiles and says 'I'm fine'. Her doctor asks her more questions. The patient says she has no hobbies. She says she has friends, however, she sounds hollow when she says this. She has sex, however, she says it doesn't mean much to her. The doctor prescribes Prozac for her 'clinical depression', or refers her to a psychiatrist who prescribes it.

Prozac is an 'anti-depressant medication' that inhibits the amount of a neurotransmitter called serotonin absorbed in a process called 're-uptake' at the synaptic gap, the place in the brain where neurons communicate with one another. About two weeks later this woman reports she feels much better. She says she never realized how depressed she was. She reports she's in touch with the 'real me'. This seems to be proof she was depressed due to a biochemical imbalance, that is, abnormally low levels of serotonin—doesn't it? The diagnosis of 'depression' is confirmed through treatment.

Consider this 'evidence' another way: In the evening I enjoy a glass or two of wine. In addition to enjoying its taste, I feel 'better' after drinking wine. Do I feel better because I have a 'wine deficiency'? If something makes us feel better does this mean we needed it?

Our 'diagnosable' clinically-depressed person, now 'successfully treated' with Prozac, *still* doesn't make those changes in her life that seemed related to her depression. She doesn't leave her husband. She doesn't change careers. She doesn't go back to school. She still has no hobbies. She still sounds hollow when she talks about her 'good' friends. She still doesn't enjoy sex. However, there's a big difference now: none of this bothers her. Now she feels 'good' in a 'bad' situation. Her doctor keeps her on Prozac for years. She likes taking Prozac: it saved her life, she says.

We have no concrete evidence her serotonin was low. No blood work was done that could indicate this. And if her serotonin level was low, we have no way of knowing whether her low serotonin caused her symptoms, now labeled 'clinical depression' or whether her 'clinical depression' caused her serotonin to be low. We do know that our emotions often modify our body chemistry. For example, if someone you love dies and you go through intense grief, there are many chemical changes in your body which accompany the grief. These chemical changes do not cause your grief: the death of your loved one causes your grief.

The woman on Prozac now uses this prescription drug to avoid coping with her life. 'Coping with her life' means exercising her free will to act, to do certain things in order to feel she is in charge of her life. Prozac, not that represented by the pronoun 'I' of this woman, is 'captain of her ship'. She uses, and is encouraged to use, a drug, by a doctor, in order to get along in life.

This is an example of drug addiction, actively encouraged by the medical profession with the full support of the government.

Drugs and Religion Are Similar Experiences

Psychologically, there's an underlying similarity between this woman who is now 'diagnosed' and 'treated' for her 'depression' and someone else who smokes cigarettes, whether tobacco or marijuana, or someone who snorts cocaine or shoots heroin. There's also an underlying similarity between people who use Prozac or marijuana to avoid coping with life and those who embrace a religion, *karma*, or fate to avoid coping with life.

There are some Christians who believe that during communion or mass they are literally eating the body and drinking the blood of Christ. There are some Jews who believe that the *moror*, in the Passover seder, is literally the 'bitterness of life'. They do not believe these things because of the power of the wafer or the wine or the power of the *moror*. We might say they believe because of the power of their own minds.

Just as there are many similarities between consumers of legal drugs and consumers of illegal drugs, so there are many similarities between drug consumers and many devotees of organized religion. They're all addicted to their literal or symbolic drugs. They may mistake the symbolic representation of something with the literal thing itself. Think of Magritte's famous painting of a pipe, with the words written underneath *Ceci n'est pas une pipe* ('This is not a pipe'). One of the dangers of using psychoactive drugs is that they may promote loss of the distinction between symbol and reality, imaginal and literal reality.

Legal drug dealers pushing Prozac proclaim that Prozac 'helps' the woman in our example to get a 'foot up in the world'. They say it enables her to do what's necessary for her to do in order for her to feel better about herself. They may agree with my opinion that certain life changes are desirable for her to feel better about herself. However, they also are likely to assert she is *unable* to motivate herself to make those changes without the drug. I disagree with their use of the word 'unable'. I think 'unwilling' is more accurate.

If this woman is not motivated enough to make the necessary changes in her life when she is unhappy, that is, when she is experiencing psychic 'pain', why would she be motivated to make those changes when her psychic pain is removed? Isn't it true that *all* of the important changes you made in your life were preceded by some experience of discomfort or 'psychic pain'?

The woman I've described is frequently *encouraged* by psychiatrists, psychologists, social workers, and other members of the 'mental health' profession to depend on a socially accepted drug in order to feel better about herself. And she is *discouraged* from depending on a socially unacceptable drug in order to feel better about herself—a drug like marijuana, for example. In other words, she is encouraged to develop a habitual use of Prozac by doctors, family, and friends. I would say that the consequence of their well-intentioned encouragement is for her to feel good in bad situations.

I'm not suggesting we should seek out painful experiences in order to make important changes in our lives. Far from it. However, what we call depression has more to do with discouragement than serotonin, and the antidote to discouragement is courage, not Prozac. Life is fraught with conflict, pain, challenge, and suffering, to be sure. Pain and pleasure, joy and sadness, fear and courage, anger and love, are all part of the yin and yang we call life.

There are many similarities between the rituals of drug use and the rituals of religion. And there are many similarities between what happens to people when they ingest certain psychoactive drugs and what happens to people when they devote themselves to certain religious practices. Isn't it remarkable that no one seems to find it odd that *religion* is routinely used to treat people for the 'disease' called 'addiction'. Religion as treatment can be overt, as practiced in AA and the various 'Twelve-Step' offshoots of AA, or it can be covert, as practiced in all the major schools of allegedly secular psychotherapy.

Drugs Have No Power over People

Drugs don't cause addiction. No thing can 'addict' any person. Moreover, addiction doesn't mean you can't control your behavior. You can always control your own behavior. Drugs are inanimate objects. They have no will or power of their own.

I know it's hard to shake the idea that drugs are bad, dangerous, and evil, and that people become addicted against their will. Why else would these people be so self-destructive? It's evidently hard to face the truth that millions of people endowed with free choice can make serious mistakes and screw up their lives.

Everything the government and the addiction treatment people have tried to do about illegal drugs and addiction has failed. We know that the 'war on drugs' isn't winnable, and we know that addiction treatment doesn't work. We are miscomprehending the meaning of dangerous drugs and addiction. Our social, legal, and clinical policies are based on this miscomprehension. Ninety percent of public discussion of drug issues takes place in a fairytale world of unreality, where drugs have the power to force themselves on hapless victims, who then develop a 'disease'.

There cannot be any such thing as a war on drugs. It's impossible! Drugs can't attack us or fight back if we attack them. Drugs are always impotent victims of people. The only war we can wage is a *war on people*. The so-called War on Drugs is really a war on drug-users, social deviants, and is thus closely akin to persecution of people because of their religion or ethnicity.

People use legal and illegal drugs like Prozac and heroin to avoid coping with their lives. The reasons people avoid coping with their lives may be judged good or bad. Addiction is the expression of a person's values. Therefore, whenever we talk or write about addiction we are dealing with an ethical issue, not a medical one. Addiction is not a disease, nor is addiction a public health problem. Addiction is a choice.

The Disease Model Is Bad Medicine

Many Native Americans (formerly known as 'Indians') experience problems-in-living associated with excessive alcohol and drug consumption. Many people in the alcohol treatment and research fields believe that Native Americans metabolize alcohol differently from people of other races and, because of some as-of-yet-unidentified physiological difference, they contend that Native Americans must be genetically predisposed to alcoholism, as well as to 'chemical dependency' in general.

In my view there's a more plausible way of explaining alcohol and drug consumption among Native Americans. They choose to drink too much alcohol and to consume drugs excessively to avoid coping with their experience of life as Native Americans in a predominantly racist, that is, anti-Native American, society. Native Americans I've known are among the first to agree with this.

Native Americans are victims of literal and metaphorical genocide. Both kinds of genocide have influenced their view of the world. Many of them have developed a philosophy of hopelessness in response to this. They have learned that no amount of effort in life would bring them reward because they were assaulted by the white man. In psychology this is known as 'learned helplessness'. They use alcohol and other drugs to avoid coping with those feelings of helplessness and hopelessness. I suspect that many whites are satisfied to keep Native Americans in this existential prison.

Asserting that alcoholism and drug addiction are hereditary diseases is one way of doing this.

Several years ago I was asked to help organize, facilitate, and speak at a conference in Edmonton, Alberta, Canada, sponsored by 'First Nations' peoples there. In Canada, many Native Americans now prefer to call themselves 'First Nations peoples'. Archie Brodsky (who has written against the disease model of addiction) and I met with Doris Greyeyes and Wayne Sowan, two First Nations leaders from the Cree tribe, and helped them assemble a panel of distinguished scholars who had long differed with what we call the disease model of addiction. This panel included Thomas S. Szasz, Patricia Erickson, Dwight Heath, Roland D. Chrisjohn, and Bruce K. Alexander, among others.

Why did the First Nations peoples want us there? Because, according to Wayne and Doris, their tribal elders instructed them to organize a conference offering alternative explanations for addiction, as well as to organize a conference offering leaders in the First Nations community new approaches to helping their people solve alcohol and drug problems based on those new explanations for addiction. The disease model of addiction and treatment based on it was, according to tribal elders, *disempowering* to First Nations people. First Nations people in disease-model treatment programs, they asserted, were misled into believing they could not control their lives—in short, they were misled into believing addiction was a disease, not a choice.

The elders were right. Treatment providers advocating the disease model of addiction ignored the social, political, and economic context within which drug use occurs. Since those factors were ignored, they were *perpetuated*. First Nations people already had terrible problems with feelings of disempowerment, caused by persecution and discrimination by the white man. Why would they want to feel even *more* helpless than they already felt?

How could viewing addiction as a disease reinforce feelings of helplessness? By convincing First Nations people they had a genetic or other physiological predisposition toward heavy alcohol and drug consumption. By convincing First Nations people that because of this mythical predisposition they could not control their behavior when they consumed alcohol and other drugs. By convincing First Nations people that abstinence is the only answer to controlling their addiction. And by convincing First Nations people to abandon their own spiritual and cultural traditions in favor of a specific form of Christianity called Alcoholics Anonymous and its various Twelve-Step offshoots.

That conference was rewarding to all who attended, including the presenters. Never before had I felt the power of cultural differences so acutely. First Nations people definitely distrust the white man—and they have good reasons for doing so. However, they also accepted us, and the meeting of the minds we experienced at that conference touched all of us in deep and personal ways. I think one of the main reasons they accepted us, in addition to the importance of the message we delivered, was because we were *invited* by them to give the message. We didn't inflict our message on them because we thought it would be good for them.

My point in telling you about this conference is this: Here we have First Nations people struggling to find new ways of helping themselves overcome problems with alcohol and drugs. They are fed up with the treatment and prevention programs based on the disease model of addiction. In addition to seeing the disease model of addiction as fiction masquerading as fact, they recognize that treatment and prevention policies based on it are socially and personally destructive. I agree completely with them.

All Pain Is in the Mind

In 1999 I traveled to London to serve as a consultant and expert witness in a defamation case involving a physician from Newquay, England. Dr. J. Patrick Hickey prescribed Diconal, a synthetic opiate containing dipipanone and cyclizine, to an amphetamine addict who subsequently crushed the tablets he had been prescribed and injected them to commit suicide. Dr. Hickey lost his license to practice medicine in the U.K. as a result and he subsequently accused a former President of the British Medical Association of defamation for things he said during a BBC television program about Dr. Hickey, broadcast in 1992.

In the U.K., prescribing heroin and cocaine is legal, both for physical problems and to maintain heroin and cocaine users labeled as addicts. In order for the defendant in this case to successfully defend himself against the accusation of defamation he had to prove that Dr. Hickey's prescription of Diconal was 'medically indefensible'. Dr. Hickey argued in court that he gave his patient Diconal to ease his psychic pain. He did this so that his patient would work on himself in Primal Therapy (a type of psychotherapy favored by Dr. Hickey), dynamic meditation, and holistic medicine. The purpose of Primal Therapy and meditation, according to Dr. Hickey, was to get to the root spiritual and psychological reasons for his patient's psychic pain—psychic pain his patient sought to ease through his use of amphetamine and other drugs.

The following two exchanges, highlighting this very different perspective on addiction I've now presented to you, took place in the High Court of Justice, Queen's Bench Division, London, on May 4th, 1999. Dr. Hickey's Barrister was Frederic Reynold. The Defendant's Barrister was Gordon Bishop. Mr. Justice Gray presided.

BISHOP: How does an addict feel this [psychic] pain? It is not withdrawal symptoms you are talking about? It is something else, this psychic pain? Is it a sharp pain in the head as if you have been hit on the head with an axe or a headache or. . . .

HICKEY: No, we are not talking of physical pain in that sense, we are talking about deep psychological pain that in fact is the cause of drug addiction and which can be worsened and brought out by taking a drug like amphetamine. In massive quantities it can, in my opinion, release and expose the patient to the experience of deep painful memories and worsen the problem. . . .

BISHOP: But it is not a physical pain? . . .

HICKEY: No, it is . . . all pain is in the mind. There is no such thing as pain in the physical body. A corpse does not feel pain. There is only pain in the mind.

BISHOP: Well, pain is caused, is it not, or may be caused by something touching or breaking the skin on part of the body and then neurosensors, I think it is, send the message up the passages which are received in the brain, so the receptors in the brain receive the messages saying that pain was being suffered which shows that there has been some injury to part of the body. Is that right?

HICKEY: Yes, but that assumes that the mind is in the brain. The mind may be separate from the body. It may operate through the brain and it may operate through the body. So it is very difficult. I think all pain is actually at the end of the day perceived in the mind.

BISHOP: So you are distinguishing the mind from the brain for these purposes?

HICKEY: Yes.

BISHOP: You are saying that the pain may be felt in the mind rather than in the brain?

HICKEY: That's absolutely correct.

BISHOP: Where is the mind for these purposes?

HICKEY: The mind is a separate level of reality, nothing to do with the physical brain.

Dr. Hickey's last-quoted remark is a bit of an overstatement. I certainly accept that there is no mind without a brain and that thoughts correspond with physical events in the brain. But the mind can exert control over the body, according to the well-known principle of 'downward causation', by which a higher level of organization can control events at a lower level (Campbell 1974; Sperry 1969).

Several days later I was on the witness stand and examined by Frederic Reynold and then cross-examined by Mr. Bishop.

REYNOLD: . . Before this particular case came your way. . . were you familiar with the concept of psychic pain?

SCHALER: Of course.

REYNOLD: In the context of drug addiction treatment?

SCHALER: Yes.

REYNOLD: Can we for the record have your understanding of what the term means?

SCHALER: I think that Dr. Hickey put it rather succinctly. . . All pain is in fact psychic pain. There can be different sources of pain. For example, two months ago my father died and I experienced a great deal of pain, psychic pain. When a dog of mine died several years ago I felt a great deal of pain, and when I went, three weeks ago, to pick up a lawn mower out of the back of my car, I pulled my back out and I experienced a great deal of pain. I experienced the pain. The 'I', and I do not mean to be esoteric here, that represented by the pronoun 'I', the mind, that which is psychic. Consciousness is what experiences pain. The origin of the pain could be from diverse sources but still it is only experienced by the mind. That is what I mean.

Psychic pain as it applies to, say, drug addiction and any number of other problems generally refers to feelings of despondency, discouragement, hopelessness, helplessness, feelings of meaninglessness, isolation, fears, any number of different types of psychic pain. We all feel them and they all have different sources. . . .

BISHOP: You mentioned the question of psychic pain, and I think you were indicating that all pain was psychic in the sense that it was 'I' who experienced?

SCHALER: That is correct.

BISHOP: Are you suggesting that all psychic pain is something which can be treated with an analgesic?

SCHALER: No, because ultimately I think one resolves these issues existentially, religiously, spiritually.

JUDGE: I am sorry, can you explain what you mean by that?

SCHALER: . . . I find that underlying many problems there are primary problems of meaning that people are struggling with in life. There are problems with fears of death [and] isolation. They are problems that are common to all people. In different cultures there are different methods for dealing with these problems. It used to be that the church dealt primarily with these problems. Historically when we saw the separation of the church and state in the United States we saw the emergence of psychiatry that seemed to correlate with that, and psychiatrists became the new priests. Then with the discovery of the spirochete bacteria for syphilis in 1900 there was a renewed interest in searching for the biological causes of discomfort—what is called schizophrenia, depression, etc. Really this biological paradigm is dominating treatment today, witness the extent to which anti-depressant drugs are prescribed for psychic pain.

JUDGE: I think Mr. Bishop's question if I recall it was whether you can treat psychic pain with an analgesic.

SCHALER: With an analgesic in the sense that aspirin is an analgesic or Advil is an analgesic—does a person feel better? If it improves the way they feel physically it will probably be palliative on a psychic level but in terms of the origin of that psychic pain I don't think it will treat it or cure it.

JUDGE: So it would be purely a palliative thing?

SCHALER: Palliative, yes. . . .

JUDGE: There would not be any sort of physiological benefit?

SCHALER: Oh, I think it would stop the pain physiologically and to the extent that stopping that pain physiologically removes the psychic pain, it would be palliative.

BISHOP: Would the psychic pain be physiological?

SCHALER: No, that would be a contradiction in terms.

BISHOP: Well, that is what I thought. But it would only remove the psychic pain if there was some physical pain which it removed in the first place?

SCHALER: I don't follow you exactly. Let us see.

BISHOP: Well, the psychic pain is in the brain, is it or in . . .

SCHALER: No.

BISHOP: . . . something outside the brain? Spirit?

SCHALER: No, the psychic refers to mind. Mind and brain are different.

BISHOP: Well, could you just explain that to me because I certainly don't fully understand that. Is not the mind part of brain?

SCHALER: No, it is not.

BISHOP: Where do we find the mind?

SCHALER: Good question!

BISHOP: Well, you are treating, you see, and Dr. Hickey was . . . on his theory he was treating a patient with a physical drug, giving it to the patient which was obviously going to have a physical effect upon that patient and upon the patient's brain?

SCHALER: True.

BISHOP: Now how is that going to affect the person's mind if the mind is not a physical thing?

SCHALER: I can't tell you what the relationship is between mind and body. I can't tell you what that is because I don't know. However, who is it that says "I feel better"? That is the mind.

That is part of the mind. When you say: "I don't know this," or "I do know this," when you say it, when I say I feel better or worse, that is the mind.

BISHOP: There are some people who might well say that is the brain saying that?

SCHALER: No, the brain is a physical structure. The brain is a physical structure.

BISHOP: And drugs are working on a physical structure?

SCHALER: I agree. I agree.

BISHOP: And when you think it is your brain operating, is it not?

SCHALER: The brain is used to think, that is correct. But the brain does not initiate action, the brain does not initiate understanding, the mind comprehends and understands.

BISHOP: We are getting into a sort of religious argument . . .

SCHALER: Well, I think it is unavoidable when we talk about behavior and drug addiction. It is unavoidable. At least this is the conclusion I have come to in all the . . . teaching and the research I have done for years. . . .

BISHOP: The problem with Diconal is, is it not, that like other opioids, it is addictive, highly addictive?

SCHALER: But now we are going back to this issue of what addictive means.

JUDGE: You want more and more. The more you have the more you want?

SCHALER: I don't think that is necessarily true and I can cite studies that show that is not true. If you would like me to cite those, I will.

BISHOP: It can have a physiological effect, can it not?

SCHALER: Of course.

BISHOP: And the physiological effect makes the body want more of it?

SCHALER: The body doesn't want anything.

BISHOP: Are you saying it is the brain wants more or the mind wants more?

SCHALER: Mind, the self. The self, the person. The person.

What we see here in this exchange are two completely different ways of viewing addiction, with completely different outcomes. The patient in this case used Diconal to commit suicide. That was an unforeseeable outcome, nevertheless, it was an activity the patient alone was responsible for. The Court, as well as the General Medical Council (GMC), construed the patient's death as the result of addiction—addiction caused by Dr. Hickey's prescribing practices, which in turn was the result of his 'misunderstanding' of addiction.

The patient was viewed by Dr. Hickey as a moral agent who sought to use drugs as a way of avoiding coping with his existential experience—What Dr. Hickey accurately termed "psychic pain." The patient was viewed by the Court and the GMC as a thing, something caused, a zombie out of touch with reality because of his addiction to drugs.

Which is the more humane and accurate way of regarding why Dr. Hickey's patient killed himself? Is it more humane to regard a person as one who makes choices, that is, based on reasons, than it is to regard a person as a thing that is caused? Clearly the latter view is used not only to absolve the person who committed suicide of responsibility for the consequences of his behavior and to assign blame to another, in this case Dr. Hickey. However, viewing people as if they are things that are caused justifies paternalism, that is, legal policies where adults are regarded by powerful others as if they are children incapable of being responsible for their choices.

The Court and the GMC's position was and is that drugs and addiction cause certain socially-unacceptable behaviors, in this case suicide. That view is consistent with American Temperance-era based alcohol prohibitionist policies—and the British are now being strongly influenced by American prohibitionist views encouraged and implemented by President Clinton and the U.S. Congress. My position is very different.

I believe behavior has reasons, not causes. Dr. Hickey was operating from a similar point of view and doing so landed him in a lot of trouble. The GMC took away his license to practice medicine. He viewed the person 'first' and the body 'second'. The GMC viewed the body first and the person second. Most people think problems-in-living are caused by drugs and addiction. That's the GMC's position. It's also an inaccurate one.

Like Dr. Hickey, I see drug use as a way of avoiding coping with problems-in-living. 'Problems-in-living' is a phrase created by psychiatrist Thomas Szasz to oppose and replace the medicalization of behavior. By problems-in-living I mean those presented in our first case here involving the woman who was prescribed Prozac; and those the tribal elders of First Nations peoples are concerned with; and those I focus on as a consultant when people come to see me for help with drug problems.

Problems-in living precede drug use. They are usually the reasons for drug use. They commonly involve some sort of interpersonal conflict. Certainly, drug use can exacerbate problems-in-living. However the problems-in-living are what need to be addressed.

As a consultant in private practice since 1973, I've witnessed over and over again that focusing on clients' drug-using behavior is no way to help them give up drugs—In fact, it often encourages drug use. That's one of the reasons why addiction 'treatment' programs fail. They are approaching their patients ass-backwards. It's only by talking about their problems-in-living and encouraging them to confront and solve those problems-in-living that the drug use subsides, and the drugs are either abdicated completely, or used in responsible moderation. If you deny the fact that people can use drugs like heroin, cocaine, marijuana, alcohol, and tobacco responsibly you'll never comprehend the true meaning of addiction, and you'll never be able to help people with the problems-in-living that lead to drug use.

My position on addiction has nothing to do with advocating the use of any of the drugs I have mentioned. I oppose the use of heroin for the same reasons I oppose the use of Prozac: I think relying on these is an existential cop-out—a way of avoiding coping with life. However, I also believe that if people want to use those drugs, if they want to cop out, they have a perfect right to do so. People have the right to put whatever ideas they want into their minds and the right to put whatever substances they want into their bodies.

12

Addiction Treatment and the First Amendment

He seemeth to be addict in the maintaining of such
superstitious ceremonies.

J. Rice (1535)

What passes as treatment for addiction is actually one or another
form of conversation. The addict talks with a group of other
addicts or with a 'therapist'. While I don't consider counseling or
psychotherapy to be medicine, I do think they can be helpful to
some people. However, so-called addiction treatment usually
involves coercion (court-ordered treatments) or religious indoctri-
nation (Twelve-Step programs), and often both.

Court-ordered Indoctrination

In 1988 I was asked by the American Civil Liberties Union of
Maryland to be a consultant for them in *Maryland v. Norfolk* (*State
v. Norfolk*, Md DistCt, No. D713675; Queen Anne's County Criminal
Case No.3588, decided March 16, 1989).

John Norfolk, then 47 years of age, was arrested for driving
while intoxicated and ordered to attend Alcoholics Anonymous
meetings. He was sentenced to 20 days in jail,which was then

suspended to 18 months of probation. Norfolk objected on the basis that he was an atheist being ordered by the state into a religious program and stopped attending AA after six meetings: "They don't talk about drinking," he said. "They talk about God 50 percent of the time. I might as well be going to church on Sundays or listening to Jimmy Swaggart." Norfolk sent the following handwritten letter to the ACLU-Md.:

> To A.C.L.U. My Name is John Norfolk. On 10/14/87 I WAS Found GuiLy of D.W.I. In Queen Anne's Co. I Was Sentenced To 20 DAYS JiAL Suspended. And 18 Mos. Probation. And Attend A.A. Meetings. I Attended 6 Meetings. Because OF My personal Religious Beliefs I stoped. Now I Have To Go To Court. Feb 8 Can you help.

Mr. Norfolk also sent the following letter to his parole and probation officer:

> 12/16/87 To DDMP Monitor & Mr. Tom Draper—P & P, This is to inform you that I don't want to attend AA meetings which is a special condition of probation because of personal beliefs. John Norfolk 12/16/87.

The state probation officer told him to "ignore the religious parts." Because he refused to attend AA meetings, Mr. Norfolk was charged with violating the conditions of probation. The late ACLU-Md. attorney Ellen M. Luff appealed the District Court's rejection of her First and Fourteenth Amendment arguments to the Circuit Court in Maryland where the state yielded and agreed to provide a secular alternative to AA.

Judge John Sause of Maryland's Circuit Court stated that the subjective nature of alcohol and drug problems made it inappropriate to coerce participation and that the state had no right to add to the 'burden' of AA members by sending to their meetings unwilling people who might be disruptive and breach anonymity (Luff 1998). Some people in AA do object to the state ordering people into their program. They say doing so disrupts the integrity of their group. They only want people there who want to be there.

When courts order someone into treatment for addiction the First Amendment of the United States Constitution is violated. The First Amendment reads "Congress shall make no law respecting an establishment of religion, or prohibiting the free exercise thereof . . ." The 'establishment' clause means that the state cannot endorse any particular religious point of view. The 'free exercise' clause means that the state cannot interfere with any particular religious point of view, including atheism.

The First Amendment protects the right to nonbelief as well as belief, (*Torcaso v. Watkins* [367 U.S. 488. 6 Led 2d 982, 81 S.Ct.1680. 1961]) and even protects the practice of "a myriad of seldom heard of, off-brand, off-beat religious concepts," (*McMillan v. State* 258 Md. 147. 265 A.2d453 [1970]).

The ACLU-Md. argued primarily on the basis of the free exercise clause. Ellen Luff didn't want to eliminate AA from the court's referral: she just wanted people to have a choice as to where they could go for help. I argued with her that the establishment clause was violated and that the ACLU-Md. should have pushed for that as a salient issue. Any link whatsoever with AA constituted 'entanglement'. Later, when Ellen Luff was dying of breast cancer, she told me she was a long-time member of AA.

The state yielded in Norfolk for good reason. They knew they were going to lose the case and that would have meant they would have had to have revamped the whole state treatment system, which was heavily dependent on AA and similar Twelve-Step programs. Most treatment programs scrape off the insurance money first and then just send their 'patients' to AA. They know AA 'works' at least as well as what they have to offer. By yielding in this specific case the State of Maryland avoided the setting of legal precedent.

Treatment Violates the Constitution

I maintain that court-ordered and state-supported addiction treatment violate both clauses of the First Amendment. Because the treatment program is a religious activity, the state is thereby endorsing a particular religious point of view. This is a violation of the establishment clause. The same is true when federal and state governments subsidize addiction treatment programs. The treatment programs are an extension of the state. This is how the state becomes entangled with religion. (See *Terry v. Adams*, 345 U.S. 461, 73 S.Ct.809, 97 L.Ed. 1152 [1953]; *Blum v. Yaretsky*, 457 U.S. 991, 102 S.Ct.2777, 73 L.Ed.2d 534 [1982]; and Opinion, *Granberg v. Ashland County*, 590 F. Supp. 1005 [1989].)

The free exercise clause is violated when a person ordered into treatment objects to being told how he or she must think. In disease-model-based treatment programs the client must 'admit' he has a disease. In Twelve-Step programs they must "turn their lives over to a higher power." The state, through its agent, AA or the treatment program, is coercing citizens into adopting a particular self-concept and identity, a specific religious world-view. The state has no business 'inside' its citizens' heads.

Addiction Treatment Is Religion

If we take a look at a typical 'individual treatment plan' such as one used in Montgomery County Maryland's "Adult Addiction Programs Outpatient Addiction Services," we see the following categories and criteria used to assess treatment success:

STATEMENT OF PROBLEM
—Alcoholism/Drug Addiction; Insufficient or inappropriate involvement in self-help groups; Denial of alcoholism/addiction, insufficient knowledge of the effects of alcohol on the systems.

STATEMENT OF GOAL
—Abstinence from alcohol and other non-prescription drugs; Acceptance of the disease and development of life-style changes that will increase the likelihood of maintaining abstinence.

ACTION PLAN/CRITERIA FOR SUCCESSFUL COMPLETION &
PROJECTED DATE/SUPPORTIVE SERVICES
—Attend ___AA ___ NA ___CA ___meetings for the first three months and a total of___ thereafter per week. Identify a sponsor within three weeks of entering the program and have one on a permanent basis within two months of starting treatment; Refer family to Alanon ___, cite the number of meetings to be attended each week ___, Refer children to Children of Alcoholics ___; Attend 12 education sessions . . . Through discussion with the client, determine if the client has accepted the disease. Short Term and Long Term.

THIS FORM MUST BE UPDATED AND SIGNED BY THE CLIENT, THERAPIST AND SUPERVISOR EVERY THREE MONTHS.

Notice the emphasis on attending AA, being abstinent rather than moderate, and 'accepting' the truth of the disease model.

The relevant cases here are these: In *United States v. Seeger* (380 U.S. 163, 13 Led 2d 733, 85 S.Ct. 850, [1965]) the court stated that the test to be applied as to whether a program or activity was religious is to enquire as to "whether the Church occupies a place in the lives of its members parallel to that filled by the orthodox belief in God in religions more widely accepted in the United States." In other words, in deciding whether Twelve-Step programs, and avowedly secular programs for that matter, are religious activities, the Court must decide if those programs 'look like a religion', in the sense of being a guide to life and having an honored position in their adherents' lives.

Addiction treatment programs clearly do occupy a place in the lives of their members parallel to that filled by the orthodox belief in God in religions more widely accepted in the United States. So do most self-help programs, even if they profess to be secular and anti-religious.

In *Dettmer v. Landon* (799 F2d [4th 1986]) the court had held that the Church of Wicca, a church practicing witchcraft, was a religion. In her argument at the District Court Ms. Luff pointed out how the history of a group in determining whether it is a religion is relevant to the court's consideration of whether a group is religious or not (*Dettmer v. Landon*, page 932). AA emerged out of an evangelical religious group known as the Oxford Group, which, according to Luff's argument, attempted to recapture the impetus and spirit of primitive Christianity.

What Makes a Religion?

In *United States v. Kuch* (288 F. Supp. 439, 444, DC, [1968]), in holding that the Neo American church was not a religion, the court noted that one claiming that a group is a religion should be able to demonstrate "belief in a supreme being, a religious discipline, a ritual, and tenets to guide one's daily existence."

However, in *Theriault v. Silber* (547 F.2d 1279, 1281 [5th 1977]), the court stated: "To the extent the Kuch includes within its test criteria the requirement that one possess a belief in a Supreme being and such criterion excludes, for example, agnosticism and conscientious atheism, for the Free Exercise and Establishment shields, that requirement is too narrow" (Luff 1998).

Belief in a supreme being is not necessary for a program to qualify as religious. Many Buddhists do not believe in a supreme being or in any supernatural entity, and yet Buddhism is always considered a religion. Clearly, Twelve-Step programs meet the criteria for religion in light of the other requirements. 'Working' the Twelve Steps is a religious discipline. Many of the activities during Twelve-Step meetings are ritualistic in nature, for example, the way people introduce themselves at meetings, the way in which people have sponsors to oversee their working of the steps, the use of 'thought-terminating clichés'. The requirement for a 'ritual' is further satisfied by the calling to order of the one-hour meetings, followed either by a speaker or a Quaker Style discussion of usually 'spiritual' topics. AA meetings are concluded by everyone saying the Lord's Prayer in unison while members stand in a circle and hold hands. The tenets to guide one's daily existence are clearly present in what are called the 'Twelve Steps' and the 'Twelve Traditions'. Step 12 counsels people to "practice these principles in all [their] affairs."

AA advocates sometimes contend that AA is spiritual, not religious. However, the courts do not recognize such a distinction in terms of the First Amendment. Moreover, many groups assert they are religions when the courts rule they are not. It's just as valid for courts to rule that groups are religious despite the fact their members assert they are not.

In *Engel v. Vitale*, (370 U.S. 421, 431, 1962), a case invalidating a school prayer statute, the Supreme Court stated that the establishment clause's

> first and most immediate purpose rested on the belief that a union of government and religion tends to destroy government and degrade religion. The history of governmentally established religion, both in England and in this country, showed that whenever government had allied itself with one particular form of religion, the inevitable result had been that it had incurred the hatred, disrespect and even contempt of those who held contrary beliefs. The same history showed that many people had lost their respect for any religion that had relied upon the support of government to spread its faith. The Establishment Clause thus stands as an expression of principle on the part of the Founders of our Constitution that religion is too personal, too sacred, too holy, to permit its 'unhallowed perversion' by a civil magistrate.

In *Granberg v. Ashland County* (590 F. Supp. 1005 [1989]) the Court stated that:

> Alcoholics Anonymous materials previously received into evidence as exhibits and the testimony of the witnesses established without a doubt that religious activities, as defined in constitutional law, were a part of

the treatment program. The distinction between religion and spirituality is meaningless, and serves merely to confuse the issue rather than to rise to a genuine issue of material fact. The court concludes that there is no genuine issue of material fact as to either coercion or religious activities in the program. The plaintiff was coerced, and religious activities were a part of the program.

Freedom *from* Religion

The establishment clause protects against entanglement of the state with religion. The state must remain neutral on matters concerning religion. Very few people realize how religious AA and similar addiction treatment programs really are. When the government gets involved by supporting and ordering citizens into these religious groups it does so at great risk to liberty for all.

The free exercise clause protects freedom of religious belief, including the right to atheism and freedom *from* religious beliefs. Many people, including those at some ACLU offices, refuse to apply the First Amendment to court-ordered and state-supported treatment programs because, even though they may be inclined to agree the programs are religious, they're viewed as religious in a good cause. Moreover, they may believe the state has a compelling interest to get people into treatment. And, of course, they believe that addiction is a disease and that treatment 'works'.

If you find yourself in a situation where you feel coerced to attend any kind of addiction treatment program you should seriously consider fighting the action on the basis of First Amendment protections and violation. More and more people have been winning these cases recently. For example, New York State's highest court declared, in a five-to-two ruling, on June 11th, 1996, that state prison officials were wrong to penalize an inmate who stopped attending the organization's self-help meetings because he said he was an atheist or an agnostic: "A fair reading of the fundamental A.A. doctrinal writings discloses that their dominant theme is unequivocally religious," the court said. "Adherence to the A.A. fellowship entails engagement in religious activity and religious proselytization" (*Griffin v. Coughlin*, 88 N.Y. 2d 674 [New York Court of Appeals, decided 11th June, 1996], 649 N.Y.S. 2d 903, 673 N.E. 2d 98, cert. denied, 65 U.S. L.W. 3458 [7th January 1997]; Conlon 1997; see also *Kerr v. Farrey*, US Court of Appeals for the 7th

Circuit, No. 95-1843—[argued January 12th, 1996—Decided August 27th, 1996, Appeal from the US District Court for the Western District of Wisconsin, No. 94-C-942—John C. Shabaz, Chief Judge]).

13

What to Do about Drugs

Freedom is not something that anybody can be given,
freedom is something people take.

James Baldwin (1961)

'Well, what would *you* do about the problem?'

I did not write this book primarily to defend any specific course
of action, but to encourage a different way of thinking. However, I
have been warned that readers might feel cheated unless I offered
my answer to the question: 'What shall we do about the drug
problem?'

Public Policy: Call off the 'War on Drugs'

From a legal point of view, I advocate the complete repeal of drug
prohibition. The war on people called 'the war on drugs' is a problem masquerading as a solution. In addition to being a stupendous
drain on taxpayers, the drug war puts millions of dollars into the
pockets of prison builders, drug enforcement agencies, and illegal
drug dealers. In fact, illegal drug dealers and drug warriors are
both committed to maintaining drug prohibition. The last thing
illegal drug dealers want to see is the repeal of drug prohibition,

139

which gives them a monopoly license to make huge profits from their business, while shutting down the competition.

Most of the crime associated with drugs arises because drugs are illegal. And most crime is associated with drugs. Repeal prohibition and crime will very substantially decline, perhaps by as much as 50 percent. There is some remaining association of criminal behavior with drug use, but that is more a matter of people with problems and prone to crime, seeking drugs, than of drug use promoting crime. When people who take drugs commit crimes, they should be caught and punished for the crimes, not for the drug use. They should never be let off or put into mental hospitals because they supposedly suffer from the make-believe disease of 'addiction'.

Repeal of drug prohibition would not stop private or government institutions from having their own drug codes. It's entirely reasonable for an airline to insist that its pilots do not take certain drugs on pain of dismissal, and the same goes for any department of the U.S. military. It's also legitimate for a hotel or restaurant to require its patrons not to consume certain specific drugs on the premises, or for government bodies which regulate streets and highways to control the use of drugs thereon, just as they control nudity or loud noises.

I oppose moves to decriminalize drugs by medicalizing addiction. This kind of proposal has been advanced by drug legalizers such as George Soros (the billionaire philanthropist) and Kurt L. Schmoke (former Mayor of Baltimore). Soros, a staunch defender of the Therapeutic State, wants to medicalize addiction and marijuana. Schmoke has said that the war on drugs should be led by the Surgeon General, not the Attorney General, which is like saying that the war on Jews should have been led by Dr. Josef Mengele, not Heinrich Himmler.

'Harm reduction', as applied to drug decriminalization measures, is usually nothing more than a euphemism for medicalization. Nothing will do short of outright repeal of drug prohibition, with all currently illegal drugs available on the free market, much as alcohol and caffeine are available now.

Public Policy: Stop Funding 'Addiction Treatment'

Many people who oppose the 'war on drugs' say that the 'solution' to the 'problem' is 'treatment'. This is baloney. Addiction treatment is a scam.

People are free to seek 'treatment' even for metaphorical diseases, but the rest of us are not obligated to pay for their treatment, or for any help or advice that might benefit them. Free 'treatment' or help is available from a range of ideologically diverse groups, including AA-style Twelve-Step programs, Rational Recovery, and SMART Recovery.

Perhaps one contributing reason people drink too much or take drugs immoderately is that they believe that 'someone' is obliged to give them whatever they happen to want. This belief is confirmed when the taxpayers 'give' them expensive 'treatment' for free. We're only helping to breed a nation of narcissists when we do this, reinforcing the drug-taker's perverted sense of entitlement.

Drug users aren't the only people who need to sober up. From a public policy point of view I think we ought to stop dumping tax dollars into 'treatment'. In addition to violating the First Amendment, public funds for treatment are a complete waste of money.

Federal law requires providers of medical insurance to include 'addiction treatment' as one of the 'illnesses' for which benefits will be paid. This law should be scrapped. Medical insurance is now more expensive, because those of us with genuine diseases have to pay for the provision of bogus 'treatment' for bogus 'diseases'. Of course, insurance companies should be free to include addiction treatment, or voodoo for that matter, but they, and we their customers, should have a choice.

Addiction is not a disease and therefore cannot be medically 'treated'. As a matter of fact, there is currently no addiction 'treatment' that has been proved effective. But of course, people should be entirely free to preach the doctrine that addiction is a disease and to offer their 'treatments', gratuitously or for payment. Just as we don't expect the taxpayers to subsidize *The Psychic Hotline*, so they should not subsidize 'addiction treatment', which is just about as scientific.

If at some future time it is ever shown that some form of counseling or therapy does 'work' in the sense of persuading people who consume drugs unwisely to moderate or cease their drug-taking, this would be interesting and fruitful, but it would not justify government support for any such professional advice-giving. As a responsible adult, you have the right to take whatever drugs you want. It's not the government's business to decide that you are making a mistake, and then get the taxpayers to subsidize someone to talk you into a different way of living your own life.

Drugs and Your Children

You are right to be concerned about the possibility (or the actuality) of your children's involvement with drugs. Similarly, you would be right to be concerned about your children's involvement with some religious group. Keep things in perspective: there are risks, of course, but most kids who get involved with drugs, like most kids who get involved with a cult, mature out of it in time, without any serious lasting damage.

Help your children to understand that delayed gratification is usually worth the wait. Show them by explanation and example that it's better to endure minor frustrations without complaint. Don't upset yourself when you don't get what you want right away. Many children and even some adults become impatient and anxious when their appetites are not instantly gratified. Explain to your children that this is how babies, not real grown-ups, behave. Grown-ups can always wait.

Show your children that you, and they, can resist temptation. Do not, for instance, say things like: 'I know I ought to lose weight but that candy bar has my name on it.' Let your children see you working calmly toward a goal, not freaking out when you meet setbacks, and then joyfully celebrating your satisfaction when the goal is reached (or serenely moving on to the next project if the goal is unfortunately not reached).

Pay close attention to how your children model your behavior. I don't mean primarily your use of drugs. Most parents don't drink excessively or use illegal drugs. I'm talking about the possible disparity between your words and deeds. Many parents think their children will learn from what they say to them. In fact their children learn more from how their parents think and behave. The example set is the lesson learned. Your actions and thoughts count for more than your explicit advice.

You may say that it's important to feel good about yourself; however, if your words and actions betray that you don't feel good about yourself, if for example, you put yourself down repeatedly with self-denigrating remarks, that's what your children will learn and copy. I know this may be very difficult for you to want to admit. But please show a little courage. They'll model that too. If you're going to be cowardly and defensive about your own problems that's what you'll end up teaching them, to be cowardly and defensive.

Praise and censure your children for what they do, not for who they are. Be careful not to equate the two. Reason with your kids; don't resort to authoritarian commands. Give evidence and reasons for what you do and say when you guide them and set rules for living.

Don't be too permissive. Many times kids create trouble because they want rules, guidance, and limits set for them. Otherwise, they feel their parents don't care about them and they feel lost in the world. Whether you like it or not, you are your kids' guru. They depend on you. It's a responsibility. Live up to it.

My general rule about responsibility with kids is this: up until the age of 18, the blame for problems with children should rest with the parents. After 18 it's the kids' fault. And don't blame your own parents for your present problems: that is no way to move on to become an autonomous individual.

I sometimes see parents relate to their children as if the kids were older than they really are. That creates big problems for them. Children, even when they seem poised and self-possessed, lack judgment in many situations, and need guidance. On the other hand, don't treat your children as if they're younger than they really are. That creates problems too. Be authoritative—not authoritarian—in your relations with them. Explain the facts, and separate facts from fiction. Explain as truthfully as you can the consequences of certain actions, and try to give an accurate, not an exaggerated, impression of the likelihood that those consequences will occur. Children need to learn about the relationship between actions and consequences.

Don't parrot the idiotic drug war propaganda to your kids. They know it's not true, and you will merely diminish your own credibility. Don't tell them that if they smoke marijuana it will lead on to heroin, and if they take heroin they will become physically unable to stop and will then die—this is all nonsense. Because the U.S. government lies and lies and lies, that doesn't mean you should repeat their lies to your children.

Get the DARE (Drug Awareness Resistance Education) programs thrown out of the public schools. All kids really learn from those programs is that good self-esteem and doing what a policeman says are somehow related. That's a terrible message for them to learn. Tell the truth to your children: don't try to scare them by wild exaggeration.

Don't go ballistic when you find out that your children have gotten drunk, smoked dope, or dropped acid. Talk to them about the facts as well as the risks of harm. None of those risks has anything to do with developing a disease called addiction. Teach them that addiction is a choice and that they have the power to exercise their will to do what they want. They have the power by their choices to destroy themselves or make something wonderful of their lives.

When kids start getting into destructive addictions it may be a way for them to avoid coping with a problem in their lives. Something their parents are doing may be a part of that problem.

I have always found it to be of tremendous value to talk about ethical dilemmas with children of all ages. Invite them to express their opinion on serious matters. And take different points of view on the matters, to help them grow out of their egocentrism. I think you'll find they enjoy talking to you about these things.

OK, So What about Me?

As a psychologist, I often counsel people who are concerned about their own excessive reliance on drugs, or are afraid that they have the potential to develop into 'addicts'.

I believe that people choose to addict themselves to drugs mainly because of unhappiness due to their problems-in-living. Many of these problems-in-living arise because people will not muster up the courage to do what needs to be done. They use drugs and get into negative addictions because they kid themselves that they can somehow solve problems by deadening themselves to those problems. People who rely on Prozac or heroin are deadening themselves, as a way of avoiding the effort and resolve required to face life's problems.

One way to begin to face your problems may be to talk to someone about them. You can do this with someone who calls herself a therapist or with someone else. All therapy boils down to one task: separating fact from fiction.

Perhaps you can help yourself by learning to become more autonomous. Spend less time socializing and being superficial with others and more time by yourself and being honest. If you're out of balance by spending too much time away from others spend more time focusing your life on being intimate with others. Take risks. For example, tell people you really care about that you love them. Stop playing it so safe.

Stanton Peele, Archie Brodsky, and Mary Arnold were on the right track when they wrote that people should consider how much they value self-control and moderation; accomplishment and competence; self-consciousness and awareness of one's environment; health; self-esteem; and relationships with others, community, and society as bedrock values against addiction (1991).

All of that is reasonable enough and there's a fair amount of research supporting the helpfulness of their suggestions. But there are limits to this helpfulness: I have met many people who value all of those things and still they get into trouble with negative addictions.

I think many people engage in self-destructive addictions because they fear death. They are also completely bewildered about what it means to be a human being and this bothers them a lot. That's why they may addict themselves to self-destructive forms of religion. That's why those who addict themselves to AA or other Twelve-Step gatherings like them so much.

People are bothered by the fact that tragedy can strike suddenly. They're bothered by the fact that bad things happen to good people and that bad people get away with murder. People are frightened of growing up, of being free and responsible. They want someone else to take over the responsibility for their lives: a parent, a god, or a drug.

When I was meditating in Punjab state, India, 24 years ago, I listened to a talk at an ashram. The speaker was giving a discourse in Punjabi. I couldn't understand a word, but I listened carefully to the rhythms of his speech and watched the faces of those listening.

All of a sudden, he spoke one sentence in English: "If you are alone in a room, sit in a corner and search your heart." When I returned to the U.S., people asked me what I had learned. I said I'd learned that I didn't need to go to India any more.

My final advice is this: don't try to remember anything I've written here. Watch *The Wizard of Oz*, the original version with Judy Garland. Dorothy, the Scarecrow, the Tin Man, and the Lion all symbolize parts of you. You're suffering, in part, because you imagine there's a wizard out there who is eventually going to give you what you think you need—a home, a brain, a heart, and courage. That's all a myth, *maya* or illusion as the Buddhists would say.

There *are* a few good wizards out there, and I'm lucky to have known some of them. What makes them good wizards is that when you have conversations with them you realize that everything you've ever really been searching for is already within you. The rest is up to you. The more responsibility you take for your own actions the more freedom you take too. You hold your life in your own hands. What you do with it is your choice.

Bibliography

Akers, R.L. 1991. Addiction: The Troublesome Concept. *Journal of Drug Issues*, 21, 777–793.

Alcoholics Anonymous World Services. 1967. *As Bill Sees It: The A.A. Way of Life . . . Selected Writings of A.A.'s Co-founder.* New York: Alcoholics Anonymous World Services.

———. 1973. *Came to Believe . . . The Spiritual Adventure of A.A. as Experienced by Individual Members.* New York: Alcoholics Anonymous World Services.

———. 1976. *Alcoholics Anonymous: The Story of How Many Thousands of Men and Women Have Recovered from Alcoholism.* 3rd edn. New York: Alcoholics Anonymous World Services.

Alexander, B.K. 1982. James M. Barrie and the Expanding Definition of Addiction. *Journal of Drug Issues* (Fall), 397–413.

———. 1987. The Disease and Adaptive Models of Addiction: A Framework Evaluation. *Journal of Drug Issues*, 17, 47–66.

———. 1990a. *Peaceful Measures: Canada's Way Out of the 'War on Drugs'.* Toronto: University of Toronto Press.

———. 1990b. The Empirical and Theoretical Bases for an Adaptive Model of Addiction. *Journal of Drug Issues*, 20, 37–65.

Alexander, B.K., R.B. Coambs, and P.F. Hadaway. 1978. The Effect of Housing and Gender on Morphine Self-Administration in Rats. *Psychopharmacology*, 58, 175–79.

Alexander, B.K., P. Hadaway, and R. Coambs. Rat Park Chronicle. *British Columbia Medical Journal*, 22, No. 2 (February).

Alexander, B.K., and A.R.F. Schweighofer. 1988. Defining 'Addiction'. *Canadian Psychology*, 29, 151–162.

Alexander, F., and M. Rollins. 1984. Alcoholics Anonymous: The Unseen Cult. *California Sociologist: A Journal of Sociology and Social Work* (Winter), 33–48.

Alksne, H., R.E. Trussell, J. Elinson, and J. Patrick. 1959. *A Follow-up Study of Treated Adolescent Narcotic Users.* Unpublished report. New York: Columbia University School of Public Health and Administrative Medicine.

American Medical Association. 1967. *Manual on Alcoholism of the American Medical Association.* Chicago: American Medical Association.

American Psychiatric Association. 1994. *Diagnostic and Statistical Manual of Mental Disorders (DSM-IV).* 4th edn. Washington, DC: American Psychiatric Association.

Antze, P. 1987. Symbolic Action in Alcoholics Anonymous. In Douglas 1987, 149–181.

Armor, D.J., J.M. Polich, and H.B. Stambul. 1978. *Alcoholism and Treatment.* New York: Wiley.

Ayala, F.J., and T. Dobzhansky. 1974. *Studies in the Philosophy of Biology: Reduction and Related Problems.* Berkeley: University of California Press.

Ayres, B.D., Jr. 1988. Atheist Challenges Order to Attend A.A. Meetings. *New York Times* (11th July).

Bailey, M.B. 1970. Attitudes toward Alcoholism Before and After a Training Program for Social Caseworkers. *Quarterly Journal of Studies on Alcohol*, 31, 669–683.

Bakalar, J.B., and L. Grinspoon. 1984. *Drug Control in a Free Society.* New York: Cambridge University Press.

Bales, R.F. 1944. The Therapeutic Role of Alcoholics Anonymous as Seen by a Sociologist. *Quarterly Journal of Studies on Alcohol*, 2, 267–278.

Bammer, G., and A. Sengoz. 1995. The Canberra Christmas Overdoses Mystery. *Drug and Alcohol Review*, 14, 235–37.

Bandura, A. 1977. Self-Efficacy: Towards a Unifying Theory of Behavioral Change. *Psychological Review*, 84, 191–215.

———. 1986. *Social Foundations of Thought and Action: A Social Cognitive Theory.* Englewood Cliffs: Prentice-Hall.

Barker, P.J., and B. Davidson, eds. 1998. *Psychiatric Nursing: Ethical Strife.* New York: Arnold.

Barnett, M.L. 1955. Alcoholism in the Cantonese of New York City: An Anthropological Study. In Diethelm 1955, 179–227.

Bateson, G. 1971. The Cybernetics of 'Self': A Theory of Alcoholism. *Psychiatry*, 34, No. 1, 1–18.

Becker, E. 1973. *The Denial of Death.* New York: Free Press.

Bennett, L.A. 1988. Alcohol in Context: Anthopological Perspectives. *Drugs and Society*, 2, 89–131.

Berger, L. 1991. *Substance Abuse as Symptom: A Psychoanalytic Critique of Treatment Approaches and the Cultural Beliefs that Sustain Them.* Hillsdale, NJ: Analytic Press.

Bergmakr, A., and L. Oscarsson. 1991. Does Anybody Really Know What They Are Doing? Some Comments Related to Methodology of Treatment Service Research. *British Journal of Addiction*, 86, 139–142.

Berzins, J.I. and W.F. Ross. 1973. Locus of Control Among Opiate Addicts. *Journal of Consulting and Clinical Psychology*, 40, 84–91.

Biernacki, P. 1986. *Pathways from Heroin Addiction: Recovery Without Treatment*. Philadelphia: Temple University Press.

Bigelow, G., M. Cohen, I. Liebson, and L.A. Faillace. 1972. Abstinence or Moderation? Choice by Alcoholics. *Behavioral Research and Therapy*, 10, 209–214.

Billings, P. 1990. The Drink Link. Interview with Robert Bazell. *New Republic* (May 7th), 13–14.

Blum, K., E. Noble, P.J. Sheridan, A. Montgomery, T. Ritchie, P. Jagadeeswaran, H. Nogami, A.H. Briggs, and J.B. Cohn. 1990. Allelic Association of Human Dopamine D_2 Receptor Gene in Alcoholism. *Journal of the American Medical Association*, 263, 2055–060.

Blumberg, L.U. 1978. The Institutional Phase of the Washingtonian Total Abstinence Movement: A Research Note. *Journal of Studies on Alcohol*, 39, 1591–1606.

Blumberg, L.U., and W.L. Pittman. 1991. *Beware the First Drink! The Washington Temperance Movement and Alcoholics Anonymous*. Seattle: Glen Abbey Books.

Boaz, D., ed. 1990. *The Crisis in Drug Prohibition*. Washington, DC: Cato Institute.

Bolos, A.M., M. Dean, S. Lucas-Derse, M. Ramsburg, G.L. Brown, and D. Goldman. 1990. Population and Pedigree Studies Reveal a Lack of Association between the Dopamine D_2 Receptor Gene and Alcoholism. *Journal of the American Medical Association*, 264, 3156–160.

Bowen, R.B. 1988. Raising Public Awareness about the Extent of Alcohol-related Problems: An Overview. *Public Health Reports*, 103, 559–563.

Bower, B. 1997. Alcoholics Synonymous. *Science News*, 151 (25th January).

Brady, M. 1993. Giving Away the Grog: An Ethnography of Aboriginal Drinkers Who Quit Without Help. *Drug and Alcohol Review*, 12, 401–411.

Brady, M. 1995. Culture in Treatment, Culture as Treatment: A Critical Appraisal of Developments in Addictions Programs for Indigenous North Americans and Australians. *Social Science Medicine*, 41, 1487–498.

Brecher, E.M. 1972. *Licit and Illicit Drugs*. Boston: Little, Brown.

Breggin, P.R. 1993. Psychiatry's Role in the Holocaust. *International Journal of Risk and Safety in Medicine*, 4, 133–148.

Breslin, F.C., S.L. Sobell, L.C. Sobell, and M.B. Sobell. 1997. Alcohol Treatment Outcome Methodology: State of the Art 1989–1993. *Addictive Behaviors*, 22, 145–155.

Brisbane, F.L. 1989. Alcoholism: From Many Perspectives. *Social Casework: The Journal of Contemporary Social Work* (June), 323–24.

Brown, D. 1991. Genetic Studies Yield Opposite Results. *Washington Post* (2nd October), A3.

Brown, H.P. and J.H. Peterson. 1991. Assessing Spirituality in Addiction Treatment and Follow-up: Development of the Brown-Peterson Recovery Progress Inventory (B-PRPI). *Alcoholism Treatment Quarterly*, 8, 21–50.

Brundage, V. 1985. Gregory Bateson, Alcoholics Anonymous, and Stoicism. *Psychiatry: Journal for the Study of Interpersonal Process*, 48, 40–51.

Bufe, C. 1998. *Alcoholics Anonymous: Cult or Cure?* 2nd edn., revised and expanded. Tucson: See Sharp Press.

Bureau of National Affairs, Inc. 1988. ACLU Aids Atheist in Challenge to A.A. as Probation Condition. *Trial Practice Series: BNA Criminal Practice Manual* (7th September), 2, 426–28.

Butts, S.V. and J. Chotlos. 1973. A Comparison of Alcoholics and Non-Alcoholics on Perceived Locus of Control. *Quarterly Journal of Studies on Alcohol*, 34, 1327–332.

Caetano, R. 1987. Public Opinions about Alcoholism and its Treatment. *Journal of Studies on Alcohol*, 48, 153–160.

Cahalan, D. 1970. *Problem Drinkers*. San Francisco: Jossey-Bass.

———. 1979. Why Does the Alcoholism Field Act Like a Ship of Fools? *British Journal of Addiction*, 74, 235–38.

———. 1988. Implications of the Disease Concept of Alcoholism. *Drugs and Society*, 2, 49-68.

Cain, A.H. 1967. Alcoholics Anonymous: Cult or Cure? In Landis 1967, 46–54.

Calicchia, J.P. 1974. Narcotic Addiction and Perceived Locus of Control. *Journal of Clinical Psychology*, 30, 499–504.

Campbell, D.T. 1974. 'Downward Causation' in Hierarchically Organised Biological Systems. In Ayala and Dobzhansky 1974, 179–186.

Carrese, J.A. and L.A. Rhodes. 1995. Western Bioethics on the Navajo Reservation: Benefit or Harm? *Journal of the American Medical Association*, 274, 826–29.

Chafetz, M. 1996. *The Tyranny of Experts: Blowing the Whistle on the Cult of Expertise*. Lanham, Md: Madison Books.

Chein, I., D.L. Gerrard, R.S. Lee, and E. Rosenfeld. 1964. *The Road to H: Narcotics, Delinquency, and Social Policy*. New York: Basic Books.

Chess, S.B., C. Neuringer, and G. Goldstein. 1971. Arousal and Field Dependency in Alcoholics. *Journal of General Psychology*, 85, 93–102.

Chiauzzi, E.J. and S. Liljegren. 1993. Taboo Topics in Addiction Treatment: An Empirical Review of Clinical Folklore. *Journal of Substance Abuse Treatment*, 10, 303–316.

Chick, J., B. Rison, J. Connaughton, and A. Stewart, 1988. Advice Versus Extended Treatment for Alcoholism: A Controlled Study. *British Journal of Addiction*, 83, 159–170.

Christopher, J. 1988. *How to Stay Sober: Recovery Without Religion.* Buffalo: Prometheus.

———. 1989. *Unhooked: Staying Sober and Drug-free.* Buffalo: Prometheus.

Churchill, J.C., J.P. Broida, and N.L. Nicholson. 1990. Locus of Control and Self-Esteem of Adult Children of Alcoholics. *Journal of Studies on Alcohol*, 51, 373–76.

Cloninger, C.R. 1991. D$_2$ Dopamine Receptor Gene is Associated but Not Linked with Alcoholism. *Journal of the American Medical Association*, 266, 1833–34.

Cohen, D., ed. 1990. Challenging the Therapeutic State: Critical Perspectives on Psychiatry and the Mental Health System. *Journal of Mind and Behavior*, 11.

Cohen, F. 1962. Personality Changes among Members of Alcoholics Anonymous. *Mental Hygiene*, 46, 427–437.

Cohen, M., I. Liebson, L. Faillace, and W. Speers. 1971. Alcoholism: Controlled Drinking, and Incentives for Abstinence. *Psychological Reports*, 28, 575–580.

Cohen, M., I. Liebson, L. Faillace, and R. Allen. 1971. Moderate Drinking by Chronic Alcoholics: A Schedule-dependent Phenomenon. *Journal of Nervous and Mental Disease*, 153, 434–444.

Conlon, L.S. 1997. *Griffin v. Coughlin*: Mandated AA Meetings and the Establishment Clause. *Journal of Church and State*, 39, 427–454.

Conrad, P. and J.W. Schneider. 1992. *Deviance and Medicalization: From Badness to Sickness.* Expanded edn. Philadelphia: Temple University Press.

Cook, D.R. 1985. Craftsman Versus Professional: Analysis of the Controlled Drinking Controversy. *Journal of Studies on Alcohol*, 46, 433–442.

Costello, R.M. and K.R. Manders. 1974. Locus of Control and Alcoholism. *British Journal of Addiction*, 69, 11–17.

Cox, W.M., ed. 1990. *Why People Drink: Parameters of Alcohol as a Reinforcer.* New York: Gardner Press.

Crawford, J. R., N.A. Thomson, F.E. Gullon, and P. Garthwaite. 1989. Does Endorsement of the Disease Concept of Alcoholism Predict Humanitarian Attitudes to Alcoholics? *International Journal of the Addictions*, 24, 71–77.

Cummings, C., J.R. Gordon, and G.A. Marlatt. 1980. Relapse, Prevention, and Prediction. In Miller 1980.

Darke, S., and D. Zador. 1996. Fatal Heroin 'Overdose': A Review. *Addiction*, 91(12), 1765–772.

Davies, D.L. 1962. Normal Drinking in Recovered Alcohol Addicts. *Quarterly Journal of Studies on Alcohol*, 23, 94–104.

Diethelm, O., ed. 1955. *Etiology of Chronic Alcoholism*. Springfield, Il: Charles C. Thomas.

Diskin, M.H., and G. Klonsky. 1964. A Second Look at the New York State Parole Drug Experiment. *Federal Probation*, 28, 34–41.

Distefano, M.K., Jr., M.W. Pryer, and J.L. Garrison. 1972. Internal-External Control among Alcoholics. *Journal of Clinical Psychology*, 28, 36–37.

Ditman, K.S., G.G. Crawford, E.W. Forgy, H. Moskowitz, and C. MacAndrew. 1967. A Controlled Experiment on the Use of Court Probation for Drunk Arrests. *American Journal of Psychiatry*, Vol. 124, 160–63.

Dodes, L.E. 1992. Review of 'Substance Abuse as Symptom'. *New England Journal of Medicine*, 326, 1368–69.

Dolan, M.A. 1988. God, the Courts, and AA. *Evening Sun* (Baltimore, 9th August), A6.

Donovan, D.M., and M.E. Mattson, eds. 1994. Alcoholism Treatment Matching Research: Methodological and Clinical Approaches. *Journal of Studies on Alcohol*, Supplement No. 12.

Donovan, M.E. 1984. A Sociological Analysis of Commitment Generation in Alcoholics Anonymous. *British Journal of Addiction*, 79, 411–18.

Douglas, M., ed. 1987. *Constructive Drinking: Perspectives on Drink from Anthropology*. New York: Cambridge University Press.

Drew, L.R.H. 1968. Alcoholism as a Self-Limiting Disease. *Quarterly Journal of Studies on Alcohol*, Vol. 29, 956–967.

Drug Policy Letter. 1996. Free Advice on Treating Alcoholics. *Drug Policy Letter*, 5 (Summer). Washington, DC: Drug Policy Foundation.

Duvall, H., B. Locke, and L. Brill. 1963. Follow-up Study of Narcotic Drug Addicts Five Years after Hospitalization. *Public Health Reports*, 78 (March), 185–193.

Eckhardt, W. 1967. Alcoholic Values and Alcoholics Anonymous. *Quarterly Journal of Studies on Alcohol*, 28, 277–288.

Edelstein, M.R., and Steele, D.R. 1997. *Three Minute Therapy: Change Your Thinking, Change Your Life*. Lakewood, Co: Glenbridge.

Edwards, G. 1985. A Later Follow-up of a Classic Case Series: D.L. Davies's 1962 Report and Its Significance for the Present. *Journal of Studies on Alcohol*, 46, 181–190.

Edwards, G., and M. Grant, eds. 1980. *Alcoholism Treatment in Transition*. Baltimore: University Park Press.

Edwards, G., J. Orford, S. Egert, S. Guthrie, A. Hawker, C. Hensman, M. Mitcheson, E. Oppenheimer, and C. Taylor. 1977. Alcoholism: A Controlled Trial of 'Treatment' and 'Advice'. *Journal of Studies on Alcohol*, 38, 1004–031.

Emerick, C.D. 1974. A Review of Psychologically Oriented Treatment of Alcoholism: I. The Use and Interrelationships of Outcome Criteria and

Drinking Behavior Following Treatment. *Quarterly Journal of Studies on Alcohol*, 35, 523–549.

Emory, P. 1988. Convicted Driver Says AA Violates Religious Rights. *Baltimore Sun* (3rd July), 1B.

Engle, K.B., and T.K. Williams. 1972. Effect of an Ounce of Vodka on Alcoholics' Desire for Alcohol. *Quarterly Journal of Studies on Alcohol*, 33, 1099–1105.

Engs, R.C., ed. 1990. *Controversies in the Addiction Field, Volume 1*. Dubuque, Ia: Kendall/Hunt.

Erickson, P.G. and G.F. Murray. 1989. The Undeterred Cocaine User: Intention to Quit and Its Relationship to Perceived Legal and Health Threats. *Contemporary Drug Problems* (Summer), 141–156.

Erickson, P.G. and T.R. Weber. 1994. Cocaine Careers, Control, and Consequences: Results from a Canadian Study. *Addiction Research*, 2, No. 1. Reprinted in Schaler 1998a.

Erickson, P.G., and B.K. Alexander. 1989. Cocaine and Addictive Liability. *Social Pharmacology*, 3, 249–270. Reprinted in Schaler 1998a, 271–287.

Erickson, P.G., E.M. Adlaf, G. Murray, and R.G. Smart. 1987. *The Steel Drug: Cocaine in Perspective*. Lexington, Ma: Heath.

———. 1994. *The Steel Drug: Cocaine in Perspective*. 2nd edn. Revision of Erickson et al. 1987. Lexington, Ma: Heath.

Escobedo, L.G., R.F. Anda, P.F. Smith, P.L. Remington, and E.E. Mast. 1990. Sociodemographic Characteristics of Cigarette Smoking Initiation in the United States: Implications for Smoking Prevention Policy. *Journal of the American Medical Association*, 264, 1550–55.

Evans, R.L., and I.M. Berent, eds. 1992. *Drug Legalization: For and Against*. Chicago: Open Court.

Faillace, L.A., R.N. Flamer, S.D. Imber, and R.F. Ward. 1972. Giving Alcohol to Alcoholics: An Evaluation. *Quarterly Journal of Studies on Alcohol*, 33, 85–90.

Farber, S. 1999. *Unholy Madness: The Church's Surrender to Psychiatry*. Downer's Grove, Il: InterVarsity Press.

Faulkner, W., D. Sandage, and B. Maguire. 1988. The Disease Concept of Alcoholism: The Persistence of An Outmoded Scientific Paradigm. *Deviant Behavior*, 9, 317–332.

Fierman, L.B. 1997. *The Therapist Is the Therapy*. Northvale, NJ: Jason Aronson.

Fillmore, K.M. 1988. Alcohol Problems from a Sociological Perspective. In Rose and Barrett 1988, 95–110.

Fillmore, K.M., and D. Kelso. 1987. Coercion into Alcoholism Treatment: Meanings for the Disease Concept of Alcoholism. *Journal of Drug Issues*, 17, 301–319.

Fillmore, K.M., and S. Sigvardsson. 1988. 'A Meeting of the Minds': A Challenge to Biomedical and Psychosocial Scientists on the Ethical Implications and Social Consequences of Scientific Findings in the Alcohol Field. *British Journal of Addiction*, 83, 609–611.

Fingarette, H. 1970. The Perils of Powell: In Search of a Factual Foundation for the Disease Concept of Alcoholism. *Harvard Law Review*, Vol. 83, 793–812.

―――. 1975. Addiction and Criminal Responsibility. *Yale Law Journal*, 84, 413–444.

―――. 1981. Legal Aspects of Alcoholism and Other Addictions: Some Basic Conceptual Issues. *British Journal of Addiction*, 76, 125–132.

―――. 1985a. Alcoholism and Self Deception. In Martin 1985.

―――. 1985b. Alcoholism: Neither Sin Nor Disease. *Center Magazine*, Vol. 18, 56–63.

―――. 1988. *Heavy Drinking: The Myth of Alcoholism as a Disease.* Berkeley: University of California Press.

―――. 1989. A Rejoinder to Madsen. *Public Interest*, 95, 118–121.

Fiore, M.C., T.E. Novotny, J.P. Pierce, A. Giovino, E.J. Hatziandreu, P.A. Newcomb, T.S. Surawicz, R.M. Davis. 1990. Methods Used to Quit Smoking in the United States: Do Cessation Programs Help? *Journal of the American Medical Association*, 263, 2760–65.

Fox, V. 1998. *Addiction, Change, and Choice: The New View of Alcoholism.* Introduction by Albert Ellis. Foreword by Jeffrey Schaler. Tucson: See Sharp Press.

Foy, D.W., R.G. Rychtarik, and B.L. Nunn. 1982. Controlled Drinking Training Effects for Chronic Veteran Alcoholics: A Randomized Trial. Paper presented at the American Psychiatric Association convention, Toronto.

Freud, S. 1959. *Group Psychology and Analysis of the Ego.* New York: Norton.

Galanter, M., ed. 1987. *Recent Developments in Alcoholism, Vol. 5*, New York: Plenum.

―――. 1989. *Cults: Faith, Healing, and Coercion.* New York: Oxford University Press.

―――. 1990. Cults and Zealous Self-Help Movements: A Psychiatric Perspective. *American Journal of Psychiatry*, 147, 543–551.

Gallup, G., and A. Gallup. 1988. Alcoholism Widely Viewed as a Disease but Opinion Diverges on Root Causes. *Gallup Poll* (24th April).

Garber, J.S., M.D. Stern, L.C. Waldman, and A. Adelson. 1989. Brief *Amicus Curiae* of the American Jewish Congress in Support of Defendant: *State of Maryland v. John Ellsworth Norfolk.* In the Circuit Court of Maryland, For Queen Anne's County, Criminal Case #3588. New York: American Jewish Congress (2nd March).

Gazzaniga, M.S. 1990. The Opium of the People: The Federal Drugstore. Interview. *National Review* (5th February), 34–41. Reprinted in Evans and Berent 1992.

Gelman, D., E.A. Leonard, and B. Fisher. 1991. Clean and Sober: And Agnostic. *Newsweek* (8th July), 62–63.

Gibbins, R.J., Y. Israel, H. Kalant, R.E. Popham, W. Schmidt, and R.G. Smart, eds. 1976. *Research Advances in Alcohol and Drug Problems, Volume 3.* New York: Wiley.

Glaser, F.B. 1980. Anybody Got a Match? Treatment Research and the Matching Hypothesis. In Edwards and Grant 1980, 178–196.

Glaser, F.B., and A.C. Ogborne. 1982. Does A.A. Really Work? *British Journal of Addiction*, 77, 123–29.

Glaser, F.B., and H.A. Skinner. 1981. Matching in the Real World: A Practical Approach. In Gottheil, McLellan, and Druley 1981, 295–324.

Glasser, W. 1976. *Positive Addiction.* New York: Harper and Row.

Glassner, B., and B. Berg. 1984. Social Locations and Interpretations: How Jews Define Alcoholism. *Journal of Studies on Alcohol*, 45, 16–25.

Glatt, M.M. 1967. The Question of Moderate Drinking Despite 'Loss of Control'. *British Journal of Addiction*, Vol. 62, 267–274.

Glynn, T.J. 1990. Methods of Smoking Cessation: Finally, Some Answers. Editorial. *Journal of the American Medical Association*, 263, 2795–96.

Gold, M.S. 1985. *800-Cocaine.* New York: Bantam.

Gomberg, E.L., H.R. White, and J.A. Carpenter, eds. 1982. *Alcohol, Science, and Society Revisited.* Ann Arbor: University of Michigan Press.

Goodwin, D.W. 1988. *Is Alcoholism Hereditary?* New York: Ballantine.

Goodwin, F.K. 1988. Alcoholism Research: Delivering on the Promise. *Public Health Reports*, 103, 569–574.

Goodwin, F.K., E. Gordis, D.L. Hardison, and L.P. Hennigan. 1988. Alcoholism Most Certainly Is a Disease. *Washington Post* (5th November), A21.

Gootenberg, P., ed. 1999. *Cocaine: Global Histories.* London: Routledge.

Gordis, E. 1995. Foreword. In Nowinski, Baker, and Carroll 1995.

Goss, A., and T.E. Morosko. 1970. Relation Between a Dimension of Internal-External Control and the MMPI With An Alcoholic Population. *Journal of Consulting and Clinical Psychology*, 34, 189–192.

Gottheil, E., A. Alterman, T.E. Skoloda, and B.F. Murphy. 1973. Alcoholics' Patterns of Controlled Drinking. *American Journal of Psychiatry*, 130, 418–422.

Gottheil, E., L.O. Corbett, J.C. Grassburger, and F.S. Cornelison. 1972. Fixed Interval Drinking Decisions, I: A Research and Treatment Model. *Quarterly Journal of Studies on Alcohol*, 33, 311–324.

Gottheil, E., H.D. Crawford, and F.S. Cornelison. 1973. The Alcoholic's Ability to Resist Available Alcohol. *Diseases of the Nervous System*, 34, 80–84.

Gottheil, E., A.T. McLellan and K.A. Druley, eds. 1981. *Matching Patient Needs and Treatment Methods in Alcoholism and Drug Abuse.* Springfield, Il: Charles C. Thomas.

Gozali, J., and J. Sloan. 1971. Control Orientation as a Personality Dimension Among Alcoholics. *Quarterly Journal of Studies on Alcohol,* 32, 159–161.

Greil, A.L. and D.R. Rudy. 1983. Conversion to the World View of Alcoholics Anonymous: A Refinement of Conversion Theory. *Qualitative Sociology,* 6, 5–28.

Grob, G.N., ed. 1981. *Nineteenth-Century Medical Attitudes toward Alcoholic Addiction: Six Studies, 1814–1867.* New York: Arno.

Gross, W.F., and V.J. Nerviano. 1972. Note on the Control Orientation of Alcoholics. *Psychological Reports,* 31, 406.

Gusfield, J.R. 1963. *Symbolic Crusade: Status Politics and the American Temperance Movement.* Urbana: University of Illinois Press.

Hadaway, P.F., B.K. Alexander, R.B. Coambs, and B. Beyerstein. The Effect of Housing and Gender on Preference for Morphine-Sucrose Solution in Rats. *Psychopharmacology,* 66, 87–91.

Hamowy, R., ed. 1987. *Dealing with Drugs: Consequences of Government Control.* Lexington, Ma: Lexington Books.

Hansen, M. 1997. Capitol Offensives. *American Bar Association Journal* (January), 50–56.

Haskell, R.E. 1993. Realpolitik in the Addictions Field: Treatment-Professional, Popular-Culture Ideology, and Scientific Research. *Journal of Mind and Behavior,* 14, 257–276.

Heath, D.B. 1989. The New Temperance Movement: Through the Looking-Glass. *Drugs and Society,* 3, 143–168.

———. 1990a. Anthropological and Sociocultural Perspectives on Alcohol as a Reinforcer. In Cox 1990, 263-290.

———. 1990b. Flawed Policies From Flawed Premises: Pseudo-Science About Alcohol and Drugs. In Engs 1990, 76–83.

Heather, N. 1992. Addictive Disorders Are Essentially Motivational Problems. *British Journal of Addiction,* 87, 828–830.

Heather, N., and I. Robertson. 1989. *Problem Drinking.* 2nd edn. New York: Oxford University Press.

———. 1981. *Controlled Drinking.* London: Methuen.

Heather, N., M. Winton, and S. Rollnick. 1982. An Empirical Test of 'a Cultural Delusion of Alcoholics'. *Psychological Reports,* 50, 379–382.

Heather, N., W.R. Miller, and J. Greeley, eds. 1991. *Self-Control and Addictive Behaviours.* New York: Pergamon.

Henderson, C.D. 1985. Countering Resistance to Acceptance of Denial and the Disease Concept in Alcoholic Families: Two Examples of Experiential Teaching. *Alcoholism Treatment Quarterly,* 1, 117–121.

Hennrikus, D.J., R.W. Jeffery, and H.A. Lando. 1996. Occasional Smoking in a Minnesota Working Population. *American Journal of Public Health*, 86, 1260–66.

Hester, R.K., and W.R. Miller, eds. 1989. *Handbook of Alcoholism Treatment Approaches*. Elmsford, NY: Pergamon.

Horgan, J. 1993. Eugenics Revisited. *Scientific American* (June), 123–131.

Horvath, A.T. 1998. *Sex, Drugs, Gambling, and Chocolate: A Workbook for Overcoming Addictions*. San Luis Obispo: Impact.

Hubbard, R.L., M.E. Marsden, J.V. Rachal, H.J. Harwood, E.R. Cavanaugh, and H.M. Ginzburg. 1989. *Drug Abuse Treatment: A National Study of Effectiveness*. Chapel Hill: University of North Carolina Press.

Hunt, G.H., and Odoroff, M.E. 1962. Follow-up Study of Narcotic Drug Addicts after Hospitalization. *Public Health Reports*, 77, 41–54.

Iannone, C. 1990. Depression-as-Disease. Review of the book, *Darkness Visible: A Memoir of Madness*. *Commentary*, November, 54–57.

Institute of Medicine, ed. 1990. *Broadening the Base of Treatment for Alcohol Problems*. Washington, DC: National Academy Press.

Jellinek, E.M. 1946. Phases in the Drinking History of Alcoholics: Analysis of a Survey Conducted by the Official Organ of Alcoholics Anonymous. *Quarterly Journal of Studies on Alcohol*, 7, 1–88.

———. 1952. The Phases of Alcohol Addiction. *Quarterly Journal of Studies on Alcohol*, 13, 673–684.

———. 1960. *The Disease Concept of Alcoholism*. New Haven: Hillhouse Press.

Jenkins, P. 1999. *Synthetic Panics: The Symbolic Politics of Designer Drugs*. New York: New York University Press.

Johnston, L.D., P.M. O'Malley, and J.G. Bachman. 1986. *Drug Use among American High School Students, College Students, and Other Young Adults: National Trends Through 1985*. Rockville, Md: National Institute on Drug Abuse.

Jones, R.K. 1970. Sectarian Characteristics of Alcoholics Anonymous. *Sociology*, 4, 181–195.

Kadden, R., K. Carroll, D. Donovan, N. Cooney, P. Monti, D. Abrams, M. Litt, and R. Hester. 1995. *Cognitive-Behavioral Coping Skills Therapy Manual: A Clinical Research Guide for Therapists Treating Individuals with Alcohol Abuse and Dependence*. Project MATCH Monograph Series Volume 3. National Institute on Alcohol Abuse and Alcoholism. Rockville, Md: U.S. Department of Health and Human Services.

Kalant, H., W. Corrigall, and W. Hall, eds. 1999. *The Health Effects of Cannabis*. Toronto: Addiction Research Foundation.

Kandel, D.B., ed. 1978. *Longitudinal Research on Drug Use: Empirical Findings and Methodological Issues*. New York: Wiley.

Kaufmann, W. 1973. *Without Guilt and Justice: From Decidophobia to Autonomy*. New York: Wyden.

Keller, M. 1972. On the Loss-of-Control Phenomenon in Alcoholism. *British Journal of Addiction*, 67, 153–166.

———. 1976. The Disease Concept of Alcoholism Revisited. *Journal of Studies on Alcohol*, 37, 1694–1717.

———. 1982. On Defining Alcoholism: With Comment on Some Other Relevant Words. In Gomberg, White, and Carpenter 1982, 119–133.

Kendell, R.E. 1965. Normal Drinking by Former Alcohol Addicts. *Quarterly Journal of Studies on Alcohol*, 26, 247–257.

———. 1979. Alcoholism: A Medical or a Political Problem? *British Medical Journal*, 1, 367–371.

Kepner, E. 1964. Application of Learning Theory to the Etiology and Treatment of Alcoholism. *Quarterly Journal of Studies on Alcohol*, 25, 279–291.

Kirkpatrick, J. 1986. *Goodbye Hangovers, Hello Life: Self-Help for Women*. New York: Ballantine.

Kishline, A. 1994. *Moderate Drinking: The Moderation Management Guide for People Who Want to Reduce Their Drinking*. Foreword by J.A. Schaler. Preface by F.B. Glaser. Introduction by S. Peele. New York: Crown.

Kissin, B. 1983. The Disease Concept of Alcoholism. In Smart et al. 1983, 93–126.

Kissin, B., and H. Begleiter, eds. 1977. *Treatment and Rehabilitation of the Chronic Alcoholic*. The Biology of Alcoholism, Volume 5. New York: Plenum.

Klausner, S.Z. 1964. Sacred and Profane Meanings of Blood and Alcohol. *Journal of Social Psychology*, 64, 27–43.

Kurtz, E. 1988. *A.A.: The Story*. Revised edn. of *Not-God: A History of Alcoholics Anonymous*. New York: Harper and Row.

Kurtz, E. and K. Ketcham. 1992. *The Spirituality of Imperfection: Modern Wisdom from Classic Stories*. New York: Bantam.

Land, E.H. 1971. Addiction as a Necessity and Opportunity. *Science*, 171, 151–53.

Landis, R., ed. 1967. *Current Perspectives on Social Problems*. Belmont: Wadsworth.

Leach, B. and J.L. Norris. 1977. Factors in the Development of Alcoholics Anonymous (A.A.). In Kissin and Begleiter 1977, 441–543.

Lefcourt, H.M., ed. 1981. *Research with the Locus of Control Construct 1: Assessment Methods*. New York: Academic Press.

Leifer, R. 1997. *The Happiness Project: Transforming the Three Poisons that Cause the Suffering We Inflict on Ourselves and Others*. Ithaca: Snow Lion Press.

Lender, M.E. and K.R. Karnchanapee. 1977. 'Temperance Tales': Antiliquor Fiction and American Attitudes toward Alcoholics in the Late 19th and Early 20th Centuries. *Journal of Studies on Alcohol*, 38, 1347–370.

Lester, D. 1989. The Heritability of Alcoholism: Science and Social Policy. *Drugs and Society*, 3, 29–67.

Lettieri, D.J., M. Sayers, and H.W. Pearson, eds. 1980. *Theories on Drug Abuse*. NIDA Research Monograph 30. Rockville, Md: N.I.D.A.

Levine, H.G. 1978. The Discovery of Addiction: Changing Conceptions of Habitual Drunkenness in America. *Journal of Studies on Alcohol*, 39, 143–174.

————. 1984. The Alcohol Problem in America: From Temperance to Alcoholism. *British Journal of Addiction*, 79, 109–119.

Lewontin, R.C. 1991. *Biology as Ideology: The Doctrine of DNA*. New York: HarperPerennial.

Lewontin, R.C., S. Rose, and L.J. Kamin. 1984. *Not in Our Genes: Biology, Ideology, and Human Nature*. New York: Pantheon.

Lieber, C.S. 1990. Alcoholism: A Disease of Internal Medicine. *Journal of Studies on Alcohol*, 51, 101–02.

Lifton, R.J. 1961. *Thought Reform and the Psychology of Totalism: A Study of 'Brainwashing' in China*. New York: Norton.

————. 1986. *The Nazi Doctors: Medical Killing and the Psychology of Genocide*. New York: Basic Books.

Ludwig, A.M., and A. Wikler. 1974. 'Craving' and Relapse to Drink. *Quarterly Journal of Studies on Alcohol*, 35, 108–130.

Luff, E. 1989. The First Amendment and Drug Alcohol Treatment Programs: To What Extent May Coerced Treatment Programs Attempt to Alter Beliefs Relating to Ultimate Concerns and Self Concept? In Trebach and Zeese 1989, 262–66.

MacAndrew, C. 1968. On the Notion that Certain Persons Who Are Given to Drunkenness Suffer from a Disease Called Alcoholism. In Plot and Edgerton 1968.

McGregor, C., S. Darke, R. Ali, and P. Christie. 1998. Experience of Non-Fatal Overdose among Heroin Users in Adelaide, Australia: Circumstances and Risk Perceptions. *Addiction*, 93(5), 701–711.

Madsen, W. 1988. *Defending the Disease: From Facts to Fingarette*. Akron: Wilson, Brown.

————. 1989. Thin Thinking about Heavy Drinking. *Public Interest*, 95 (Spring), 112–18.

Madsen, W., D. Berger, F.R. Bremy, and D.G. Mook. 1990. Alcoholism a Myth? *Skeptical Inquirer*, 14 (Summer), 440–42.

Maltzman, I. 1989. A Reply to Cook, 'Craftsman Versus Professional: Analysis of the Controlled Drinking Controversy'. *Journal of Studies on Alcohol*, 50, 466–472.

————. 1991. Is Alcoholism a Disease? A Critical Review of a Controversy. *Integrative Physiological and Behavioral Science*, 26, 200–210.

Mann, M. 1965. *Marty Mann's New Primer on Alcoholism: How People Drink, How to Recognize Alcholics, and What to Do about Them*. New York: Holt, Rinehart and Winston.

Marks, J. 1985. Opium, the Religion of the People. *Lancet* (22nd June).

Marlatt, G.A. 1983. The Controlled-Drinking Controversy: A Commentary. *American Psychologist*, 38, 1097–1110.

Marlatt, G.A., B. Deming, and J.B. Reid. 1973. Loss-of-Control Drinking in Alcoholics: An Experimental Analogue. *Journal of Abnormal Psychology*, 81, 233–241.

Marlatt, G.A., and J.R. Gordon. 1985. *Relapse Prevention: Maintenance Strategies in the Treatment of Addictive Behaviors*. New York: Guilford Press.

Martin, M.W., ed. 1985. *Self-Deception and Self-Understanding: New Essays in Philosophy and Psychology*. Lawrence, Ks: University of Kansas Press, 52–67.

Mattson, M.E., and R.K. Fuller. 1997. Reply from NIAAA. Letter to the Editor. *Epikrisis*, 8, 2.

McClelland, D.C., W.N. Davis, R. Kalin, and E. Wanner. 1972. *The Drinking Man: Alcohol and Human Motivation*. New York: Free Press.

McCrady, B.S., and S. Irvine. 1989. Self-Help Groups. In Hester and Miller 1989, 153-169.

McGrath, E., G.P. Keita, B.R. Strickland, and N.F. Russo. 1990. *Women and Depression: Risk Factors and Treatment Issues: Final Report of the American Psychological Association Task Force on Women and Depression*. Washington, DC: American Psychological Association.

Mello, N.K., and J.H. Mendelson. 1972. Drinking Patterns during Work-contingent and Noncontingent Alcohol Acquisition. *Psychosomatic Medicine*, 34, 139–164.

Menninger, K., and T.S. Szasz. 1989. Reading Notes. *Bulletin of the Menninger Clinic*, 53, 350–52.

Merry, J. 1966. The 'Loss-of-Control' Myth. *Lancet*, 1, 1257–58.

Milam, J. R., and K. Ketcham. 1983. *Under the Influence: A Guide to the Myths and Realities of Alcoholism*. New York: Bantam.

Mill, J.S. 1988 [1859]. *On Liberty*. New York: Viking Penguin.

Miller, N.S. and J.C. Mahler. 1991. Alcoholics Anonymous and the 'AA' Model for Treatment. *Alcoholism Treatment Quarterly*, 8, 39–51.

Miller, W.R., ed. 1980. *The Addictive Behaviors*. Oxford: Pergamon.

———. 1983. Controlled Drinking: A History and Critical Review. *Journal of Studies on Alcohol*, 44, 68–83.

Miller, W. R., and G.R. Caddy. 1977. Abstinence and Controlled Drinking in the Treatment of Problem Drinkers. *Journal of Studies on Alcohol*, 38, 986–1003.

Miller, W.R., and N.K. Heather, eds. 1986. *Treating Addictive Behaviors: Processes of Change*. New York: Plenum.

Miller, W.R. and R.K. Hester. 1986. The Effectiveness of Alcoholism Treatment: What the Research Reveals. In Miller and Heather 1986, 121–174.

Miller, W.R., A. Zweben, C.C. DiClemente, and R.G. Rychtarik. 1995. *Motivational Enhancement Therapy Manual: A Clinical Research Guide for Therapists Treating Individuals with Alcohol Abuse and Dependence.* Project MATCH Monograph Series Volume 2. National Institute on Alcohol Abuse and Alcoholism. Rockville, Md: U.S. Department of Health and Human Services.

Morgenstern, J. and B.S. McCrady. 1992. Curative Factors in Alcohol and Drug Treatment: Behavioral and Disease Model Perspectives. *British Journal of Addiction*, 87, 901–912.

Mitscherlich, A., and F. Mielke. 1949. *Doctors of Infamy: The Story of Nazi Medical Crimes.* New York: Henry Schuman.

Mulford, H.A. 1984. Rethinking the Alcohol Problem: A Natural Processes Model. *Journal of Drug Issues*, 14, 31–43.

Mulford, H.A., and D.E. Miller. 1964. Measuring Public Acceptance of the Alcoholic as a Sick Person. *Quarterly Journal of Studies on Alcohol*, 25, 314–323.

Murray, F.J. 1996. Courts Hit Sentencing DWIs to AA, Fault Religious Basis. *Washington Times* (4th November), A10.

Musto, D.F. 1987. *The American Disease: Origins of Narcotic Control,* Expanded edn. New York: Oxford University Press.

———. 1991. Opium, Cocaine, and Marijuana in American History. *Scientific American*, 265(1).

National Council on Alcoholism, Criteria Committee. 1972. Criteria for the Diagnosis of Alcoholism. *Annals of Internal Medicine*, 77, 249–258.

Nowicki, S., Jr., and A.E. Hopper. 1974. Locus of Control Correlates in an Alcoholic Population. *Journal of Consulting and Clinical Psychology*, 42, 735.

Nowinski, J., S. Baker, and K. Carroll. 1995. *Twelve Step Facilitation Therapy Manual: A Clinical Research Guide for Therapists Treating Individuals with Alcohol Abuse and Dependence.* National Institute on Alcohol Abuse and Alcoholism. Project MATCH Monograph Series, Volume I. Rockville, Md: U.S. Department of Health and Human Services.

O'Connell, T. 1991. Michigan Historian: Spirituality at the Heart of AA's Success. *U.S. Journal of Drug and Alcohol Dependence*, 15 (November), 2.

O'Donnell, J.A. 1964. A Follow-up of Narcotic Addicts. *American Journal of Orthopsychiatry*, 34, 948–954.

Orwell, G. 1981 [1949]. *Nineteen Eighty-Four.* New York: New American Library.

Paredes, A., W.R. Hood, H. Seymour, and M. Gollob. 1973. Loss-of-Control in Alcoholism: An Investigation of the Hypothesis with Experimental Findings. *Quarterly Journal of Studies on Alcohol*, 34, 1146–161.

Pattison, E.M. 1966. A Critique of Alcoholism Treatment Concepts with Special Reference to Abstinence. *Quarterly Journal of Studies on Alcohol*, 27, 49-71.

———. 1976. Nonabstinent Drinking Goals in the Treatment of Alcoholics. In Gibbins et al. 1976, 401–455.

Pattison, E.M., M.B. Sobell, and L.C. Sobell. 1977. *Emerging Concepts of Alcohol Dependence*. New York: Springer.

Peele, S. 1989. *Diseasing of America: Addiction Treatment Out of Control*. Lexington, Ma: Lexington Books.

———. 1997. Bait and Switch in Project MATCH: What NIAAA Research Actually Shows about Alcohol Treatment. *Psychnews International*, 2 (May-June). <http://mentalhelp.net/pni/pni23b.htm>

Peele, S., and A. Brodsky. 1975. *Love and Addiction*. Scarborough, Ontario: New American Library of Canada.

Peele, S., A. Brodsky, and M. Arnold. 1991. *The Truth about Addiction and Recovery: The Life Process Program for Outgrowing Destructive Habits*. New York: Simon and Schuster.

Perls, F.S. 1947. *Ego, Hunger, and Aggression: A Revision of Freud's Theory and Method*. London: Allen and Unwin.

———. 1969. *Ego, Hunger, and Agression: The Beginning of Gestalt Therapy*. New York: Random House.

Perls, F.S., R. Hefferline, and P. Goodman. 1951. *Gestalt Therapy: Excitement and Growth in the Human Personality*. New York: Julian.

Petrunik, M.G. 1972. Seeing the Light: A Study of Conversion to Alcoholics Anonymous. *Journal of Voluntary Action Research*, 1, 30–38.

Playfair, W.L. 1991. *The Useful Lie*. Wheaton: Good News.

Plot, S., and R. Edgerton, eds. Date 1968. *New Concepts in Mental Illness*. New York: Doubleday.

Polich, J.M., D.J. Armor, and H.B. Braiker. 1981. *The Course of Alcoholism: Four Years after Treatment*. New York: Wiley.

Prince, J. M., M.M. Glatt, H. Pullar-Strecker. 1966. The 'Loss of Control' Myth. Letters to the editor. *Lancet* (25th June), 1423–24.

Project MATCH Research Group. 1993. Project MATCH: Rationale and Methods for a Multisite Clinical Trial Matching Patients to Alcoholism Treatment. *Alcoholism: Clinical and Experimental Research*, 17, 1130-1145.

Project MATCH Research Group. 1997a. Matching Alcoholism Treatment to Client Heterogeneity: Project MATCH Post-Treatment Drinking Outcomes. *Journal of Studies on Alcohol*, 58(1), 7–29.

———. 1997b. Project Match Executive Summary. Bethesda, Md: NIAA.

————. 1998. Matching Alcoholism Treatments to Client Heterogeneity: Treatment Main Effects and Matching Effects on Drinking during Treatment. *Journal of Studies on Alcohol,* 59, 631–39.

Rank, O. 1964. *Truth and Reality.* New York: Norton.

Rather, B.C. 1991. Disease Versus Social-Learning Models of Alcoholism in the Prediction of Alcohol Problem Recognition, Help-Seeking, and Stigma. *Journal of Drug Education,* 21, 119–132.

Reinarman, C., and H.G. Levine, eds. 1997. *Crack in America: Demon Drugs and Social Justice.* Berkeley: University of California Press.

Religious News Service. 1988. Sexual Behavior Likened to Addiction. *Washington Post* (2nd April), C11.

Rice, O.R. 1944. The Contribution of the Minister to the Treatment of the Alcoholic. *Quarterly Journal of Studies on Alcohol,* 5, 250–56.

Ringwalt, C., S.T. Ennett, and K.D. Holt. 1991. An Outcome Evaluation of Project DARE (Drug Abuse Resistance Education). *Health Education Resarch Theory and Practice,* 6, 327–337.

Riply, H.S., and J.K. Jackson. 1959. Therapeutic Factors in Alcoholics Anonymous. *American Journal of Psychiatry,* 116, 44–50.

Robins, L.N., J.E. Helzer, and D.H. Davis. 1975. Narcotic Use in Southeast Asia and Afterward: An Interview Study of 898 Vietnam Returnees. *Archives of General Psychiatry,* 32, 955–961.

Robins, L.N., J.E. Helzer, M. Hesselbrock, and E. Wish. 1980. Vietnam Veterans Three Years After Vietnam: How Our Study Changed Our View of Heroin. *Yearbook of Substance Use and Abuse* (New York: Plenum), Vol. 2, 213–230.

Robinson, D. 1972. The Alcohologist's Addiction: Some Implications of Having Lost Control Over the Disease Concept of Alcoholism. *Quarterly Journal of Studies on Alcoholism,* 33, 1028–042.

Robitscher, J. 1980. *The Powers of Psychiatry.* New York: Houghon Mifflin.

Rohsenow, D.J., and M.R. O'Leary. 1978. Locus of Control Research on Alcoholic Populations: A Review. I. Development, Scales, and Treatment. *International Journal of the Addictions,* 13, 55–78.

Roizen, R. 1987. The Great Controlled-Drinking Controversy. In Galanter 1987, 245–279.

Roizen, R., D. Cahalan, and P. Shanks. 1978. 'Spontaneous Remission' among Untreated Problem Drinkers. In Kandel 1978, 197–221.

Room, R. 1983. Sociological Aspects of the Disease Concept of Alcoholism. In Smart et al. 1983, 47–91.

Rose, R.M., and J. Barrett, eds. 1988. *Alcoholism: Origins and Outcomes.* New York: Raven Press.

Rosenbaum, M., A. Washburn, K. Knight, M. Kelley, and J. Irwin. 1996. Treatment as Harm Reduction, Defunding as Harm Maximization: The Case of Methadone Maintenance. *Journal of Psychoactive Drugs,* 28(3), 241–49.

Rudy, D.R. 1986. *Becoming Alcoholic: Alcoholics Anonymous and the Reality of Alcoholism*. Carbondale: Southern Illinois University Press.

Rush, B. 1799. Observations Intended to Favour a Supposition that the Black Color (as It Is Called) of the Negroes is Derived from the LEPROSY. *Transactions of the American Philosophical Society*, 4, 289–297.

———. 1981 [1814]. An Inquiry Into the Effects of Ardent Spirits upon the Human Body and Mind, With an Account of the Means of Preventing and of the Remedies for Curing Them. 8th edn. In Grob 1981.

Sadler, P.O. 1977. The 'Crisis Cult' as a Voluntary Association: An Interactional Approach to Alcoholics Anonymous. *Human Organization*, 36, 207–210.

Sanchez-Craig, M. 1980. Random Assignment to Abstinence or Controlled Drinking in a Cognitive-Behavioral Program: Short-Term Effects on Drinking Behavior. *Addictive Behaviors*, 5, 59–65.

Sanchez-Craig, M., H.M. Annis, A.R. Bornet, and K.R. MacDonald. 1984. Random Assignment to Abstinence and Controlled Drinking: Evaluation of a Cognitive-Behavioral Program for Problem Drinkers. *Journal of Consulting and Clinical Psychology*, 52, 390–403.

Sanchez-Craig, M., R. Davila, and G. Cooper. 1996. A Self-Help Approach for High-Risk Drinking: Effect of an Initial Assessment. *Journal of Consulting and Clinical Psychology*, 64, 694–700.

Schaler, J.A. 1988a. Alcoholism Is Not a Disease. *Washington Post* (25th October), A26.

———. 1988b. Police Officers as Psychologists? I Think Not. *Montgomery Journal* (Maryland, 22nd December), A16.

———. 1989a. Alcoholism as Willful Misconduct. *Journal of the American Medical Association*, 261, 864–65.

———. 1989b. Is Addiction Treatment 'Fundamental'? *U.S. Journal of Drug and Alcohol Dependence*, 13 (July), 5.

———. 1989c. Often, Kids' Drug Abuse is Learned from Unaware Parents. *Montgomery Journal* (Maryland, 11th January), A9.

———. 1989d. Drug Use Is a Choice, Not a Disease. Letters to the Editor. *Washington Post* (26th June), A10.

———. 1989e. Don't Be Fooled by the Marketing Myth of Addictive Diseases. *Montgomery Journal* (Maryland, 4th August), A6.

———. 1989f. The Final Solution to the Drug Problem. *Baltimore Sun* (30th September), 9A.

———. 1990a. Alcoholism, Disease, and Myth. Review of Fingarette, 'Heavy Drinking'. *Skeptical Inquirer*, 14, 198–201.

———. 1990b. Alcoholism: Disease or Not? *Skeptical Inquirer*, 15 (Fall), 108.

————. 1991. Drugs and Free Will. *Society*, 28, 42–49

————. 1994. Foreword. In Kishline 1994.

————. 1995a. The Addiction Belief Scale. *International Journal of the Addictions*, 30, 117–134.

————. 1995b. Cult-Busting. *Interpsych Newsletter*, Vol. 2, No. 5 (June). <http://userpage.FU-Berlin.de/~expert/IPN/ipn2_5d2.html>

————. 1995c. 'Moderate Drinking' Programs: A Challenge to Abstinence-based Beliefs. *Epikrisis: Newsletter of the N.C. Governor's Institute on Alcohol and Substance Abuse*, Vol. 6, No. 7 (July), 4.

————. 1996a. Spiritual Thinking in Addiction Treatment Providers: The Spiritual Belief Scale. *Alcoholism Treatment Quarterly*, 14, 7–33.

————. 1996b. Thinking about Drinking: The Power of Self-fulfilling Prophecies. *International Journal of Drug Policy*, 7, 187–192.

————. 1996c. Freedom, Psychiatry, and Responsibility. *Psychnews International*, 1 (4) (July). <http://mentalhelp.net/pni/pni14b.htm>

————. 1996d. Selling Water by the River: The Project MATCH Cover-up. *Psychnews International*, 1(5) (August-September). <http://mentalhelp.net/pni/pni15c.htm>

————. 1997a. The Case Against Alcoholism as a Disease. In Shelton and Edwards 1997, 21–49.

————. 1997b. Addiction Beliefs of Treatment Providers: Factors Explaining Variance. *Addiction Research*, 4, 367–384.

————. 1997c. Critic of Project MATCH. Letters to the Editor. *Epikrisis: Newsletter of the N.C. Governor's Institute on Alcohol and Substance Abuse*, 8, 2.

————. 1997d. It's Wrong to Let Smokers Hide Behind the Excuse of Addiction. *Houston Chronicle* (30th March), 1C.

————. 1997e. Smoking and Quitting Are Matters of Free Will. Op-ed. *Minnesota Star Tribune* (April).

————. 1997f. Smoking Right and Responsibility. *Psychnews International*, 2(2) (February-March). <http://mentalhelp.net/pni/pni22b.htm> Reprinted in Schaler and Schaler 1998, 332–35.

————., ed. 1998a. *Drugs: Should We Legalize, Decriminalize, or Deregulate?* Amherst, NY: Prometheus.

————. 1998b. Moderation Management Über Alles. *Psychnews International*, 3(2) (July). <http://mentalhelp.net/pni/pni32.htm>

————. 1998c. Commentary on Sanua's 'Prescription Privileges'. *Journal of Universal Peer Review*. <http://www.enabling.org/ia/szasz/schaler/sanuacomment.html>

————. 1998d. The Meaning of Depression. Letters. *New Yorker* (9th February).

Schaler, J.A. and M.E. Schaler, eds. 1998. *Smoking: Who Has the Right?* Amherst, NY: Prometheus.

Schenk, S., G. Lacelle, K. Gorman, and Z. Amit. 1987. Cocaine Self-Administration in Rats Influenced by Environmental Conditions: Implications for the Etiology of Drug Abuse. *Neuroscience Letters*, 81, 227–231.

Schmoke, K.L. 1988. Decriminalizing Drugs: It Just Might Work—And Nothing Else Does. *Washington Post* (15th May), Outlook, B1. 1990.

———. An Argument in Favor of Decriminalization. *Hofstra Law Review*, 18, 501–525.

Searles, J.S. 1993. Science and Fascism: Confronting Unpopular Ideas. *Addictive Behaviors*, 18, 5–8.

Seligman, M.E.P. 1975. *Helplessness: On Depression, Development, and Death*. New York: Freeman.

Sells, S.B. 1981. Matching Clients to Treatments: Problems, Preliminary Results, and Remaining Tasks. In Gottheil, McLellan, and Druley 1981, 33–50.

Sessions, P.M. 1957. Ego Religion and Superego Religion in Alcoholics. *Quarterly Journal of Studies on Alcohol*, 18, 121–25.

Sharma, S.L. 1995. *The Therapeutic Dialogue: A Guide to Humane and Egalitarian Psychotherapy*. Northvale, NJ: Jason Aronson.

Shelton, W., and R.B. Edwards, eds. 1997. *Values, Ethics, and Alcoholism*. Greenwich, Ct: JAI Press.

Shiffman, S., and T.A. Wills, eds. 1985. *Coping and Substance Use*. New York: Academic Press.

Siegel, R.K. 1984. Cocaine and the Privileged Class: A Review of Historical and Contemporary Images. *Advances in Alcohol and Substance Abuse*, 4, 37–49.

Skolnick, J.H. 1958. Religious Affiliation and Drinking Behavior. *Quarterly Journal of Studies on Alcohol*, 19, 452–470.

SMART Recovery, Inc. 1996. Official literature. Available through SMART Recovery Inc., 24000 Mercantile Road, Beachwood, Ohio 44122.

Smart, R.G. 1976. Spontaneous Recovery in Alcoholics: A Review and Analysis of the Available Literature. *Drug and Alcohol Dependence*, 1, 227–285.

Smart, R.G., F.B. Glaser, Y. Israel, H. Kalant, R.E. Popham, and W. Schmidt, eds. 1983. *Research Advances in Alcohol and Drug Problems*, 7. New York: Plenum.

Smith, C.K. 1992. State Compelled Spiritual Revelation: The First Amendment and Alcoholics Anonymous as a Condition of Drunk Driving Probation. *William and Mary Bill of Rights Journal*, 1, 299–329.

Smith, D., L. Leake, J.R. Lofflin, and D. Yealy. 1992. Is Admission after Intravenous Heroin Overdose Necessary? *Annals of Emergency Medicine*, 21(11), 1326–330.

Sobell, L.C., J.A. Cunningham, and M.B. Sobell. 1996. Recovery from Alcohol Problems with and without Treatment: Prevalence in Two

Population Surveys. *American Journal of Public Health*, 86, No. 7, 966–972.

Sobell, L.C., M.B. Sobell, and W.C. Christelman. 1972. The Myth of 'One Drink'. *Behavioural Research and Therapy*, 10, 119–123.

Sobell, L.C., M.B. Sobell, T. Toneatto. 1991. Recovery from Alcohol Problems Without Treatment. In Heather, Miller, and Greeley 1991.

Sobell, M.B., and L.C. Sobell. 1989. Moratorium on Maltzman: An Appeal to Reason. *Journal of Studies on Alcohol*, 50, 473–480.

Spector, M. 1977. Legitimizing Homosexuality. *Society*, 14, 52–56.

Sperry, R.W. 1969. A Modified Concept of Consciousness. *Psychological Review*, 76, 532–36.

Sporer, K.A. 1999. Acute Heroin Overdose. *Annals of Internal Medicine*, 130, 584–590.

Spotts, J.V. and F.C. Shontz. 1980. *Cocaine Users: A Representative Case Approach*. New York: Free Press.

Stein, H.F. 1985. Alcoholism as Metaphor in American Culture: Ritual Desecration as Social Integration. *Ethos*, Vol. 13, No. 3, 195–235.

Sterk, C.E. 1999. *Fast Lives: Women Who Use Crack Cocaine*. Philadelphia: Temple University Press.

Stewart, D.A. 1954. The Dynamics of Fellowship as Illustrated in Alcoholics Anonymous. *Quarterly Journal of Studies on Alcohol*, 16, 251–262.

Strassberg, D.S. and J.S. Robinson. 1974. Relationship Between Locus of Control and Other Personality Measures in Drug Users. *Journal of Consulting and Clinical Psychology*, 42, 744–45.

Strecher, V.J., B.M. DeVellis, M.H. Becker, and I.M. Rosenstock. 1986. The Role of Self-Efficacy in Achieving Health Behavior Change. *Health Education Quarterly*, 13, 73–91.

Sullum, J. 1998 *For Your Own Good: The Anti-Smoking Crusade and the Tyranny of Public Health*. New York: Free Press.

Szasz, T.S. 1965. *The Ethics of Psychoanalysis: The Theory and Method of Autonomous Psychotherapy*. New York: Basic Books.

———. 1967. Alcoholism: A Socio-Medical Perspective. *Washington Law Journal*, 6, 255–268.

———. 1970. *The Manufacture of Madness: A Comparative Study of the Inquisition and the Mental Health Movement*. New York: Harper and Row.

———. 1972. Bad Habits Are Not Diseases. *Lancet* (8th July), 83–84.

———. 1985 [1973]. *Ceremonial Chemistry: The Ritual Persecution of Drugs, Addicts, and Pushers*. Homes Beach, Fl: Learning Publications.

———. 1987. *Insanity: The Idea and Its Consequences*. New York: Wiley.

———. 1988a. *Psychiatric Justice*. Syracuse: Syracuse University Press.

———. 1988b. *The Myth of Psychotherapy*. Syracuse: Syracuse University Press.

————. 1989a. *Law, Liberty, and Psychiatry*. Syracuse: Syracuse University Press.

————. 1989b. Thomas Szasz: The Politics of Addiction. Interview with Andrew Meacham. *Focus* (October), 10–13.

————. 1990. *The Untamed Tongue: A Dissenting Dictionary*. La Salle: Open Court.

————. 1991. Diagnoses Are Not Diseases. *Lancet*, 338 (21st–28th December), 1574–76.

————. 1992. *Our Right to Drugs: The Case for a Free Market*. Westport, Ct: Praeger.

————. 1994. Diagnosis in the Therapeutic State. *Liberty* (September), 7, 25–28.

————. 1996. *The Meaning of Mind: Language, Morality, and Neuroscience*. Westport, Ct: Praeger.

Tabakoff, B., and P. Hoffman. 1988. Genetics and Biological Markers of Risk for Alcoholism. *Public Health Reports*, 103, 690–98.

Tate, P. 1997. *Alcohol: How to Give It Up and Be Glad You Did*. 2nd edn. Tucscon: See Sharp Press.

Teal, D. 1971. *The Gay Militants*. New York: Stein and Day.

Thune, C.E. 1977. Alcoholism and the Archetypal Past: A Phenomenological Perspective on Alcoholics Anonymous. *Journal of Studies on Alcohol*, 38, 75–88.

Tiebout, H.M. 1953. Surrender versus Compliance in Therapy: With Special Reference to Alcoholism. *Quarterly Journal of Studies on Alcohol*, 14, 58–68.

Travis, C.B. 1988. *Women and Health Psychology: Biomedical Issues*. Hillsdale, NJ: Erlbaum.

Trebach, A.S. 1982. *The Heroin Solution*. New Haven: Yale University Press.

————. 1987. *The Great Drug War*. New York: Macmillan.

Trebach, A.S., and J.A. Inciardi. 1993. *Legalize It? Debating American Drug Policy*. Washington, DC: American University Press.

Trebach, A.S., and K.B. Zeese, eds. 1989. *Drug Policy 1989–90: A Reformer's Catalogue*. Washington, DC: Drug Policy Foundation.

————. 1992. *Friedman and Szasz on Liberty and Drugs: Essays on the Free Market and Prohibition*. Washington, DC: Drug Policy Foundation.

Trice, H.M. 1957. A Study of the Process of Affiliation with Alcoholics Anonymous. *Quarterly Journal of Studies on Alcohol*, 18, 39–54.

————. 1959. The Affiliative Motive and Readiness to Join Alcoholics Anonymous. *Quarterly Journal of Studies on Alcohol*, 20, 313–320.

Trimpey, J. 1989. *Rational Recovery from Alcoholism: The Small Book*. Lotus, Ca: Lotus Press.

————. 1994. *The Final Fix for Alcohol and Drug Dependence: AVRT (Addictive Voice Recognition Technique)*. Lotus, Ca: Lotus Press.

Trotter, T. 1813. *An Essay, Medical, Philosophical, and Chemical, on Drunkenness, and Its Effects on the Human Body.* Boston: Bradford and Read.

Tuchfeld, B. 1981. Spontaneous Remission in Alcoholics. *Journal of Studies on Alcohol*, 42, 626–641.

Vaillant, G.E. 1965. A Twelve-Year Follow-Up of New York Narcotic Addicts: I. The Relation of Treatment to Outcome. *American Journal of Psychiatry*, 122, 727–737.

———. 1983. *The Natural History of Alcoholism.* Cambridge, Ma: Harvard University Press.

———. 1990. We Should Retain the Disease Concept of Alcoholism. *Harvard Medical School Mental Health Letter*, 6 (March), 4–6.

Vatz, R.E., and L.S. Weinberg. 1990. The Conceptual Bind in Defining the Volitional Component of Alcoholism: Consequences for Public Policy and Scientific Research. *Journal of Mind and Behavior*, 11, 531–544.

Verbrugge, L.M. 1985. Gender and Health: An Update on Hypotheses and Evidence. *Journal of Health and Social Behavior*, 26, 156–182.

Verden, P., D.N. Jackson, and G.A. King. 1969. Popular Conceptions of the Etiology of Alcoholism. *Quarterly Journal of Studies on Alcohol*, 30, 78–92.

Waldorf, D. 1973. *Careers in Dope.* Englewood Cliffs, NJ: Prentice-Hall.

———. 1983. Natural Recovery from Opiate Addiction: Some Social-Psychological Processes of Untreated Recovery. *Journal of Drug Issues*, Vol. 13, 255–56.

Waldorf, D., C. Reinarman, and S. Murphy. 1991. *Cocaine Changes: The Experience of Using and Quitting.* Philadelphia: Temple University Press.

Wallace, J. 1993a. Fascism and the Eye of the Beholder: A Reply to J.S. Searles on the Controlled Intoxication Issue. *Addictive Behaviors*, 18, 239–251.

———. 1993b. Letter to the editors. *Addictive Behaviors*, 18, 1–4.

Wallston, K.A. 1992. Hocus-Pocus, the Focus Isn't Strictly on Locus: Rotter's Social Learning Theory modified for Health. *Cognitive Therapy and Research*, 16, 183–199.

Wallston, K.A., B.S. Wallston, and R. DeVellis. 1978. Development of the Multidimensional Health Locus of Control (MHLC) Scales. *Health Education Monographs*, 6, 160–170.

Ward, A. 1992. The Disease Defense. *Washington Post* (3rd December), A21.

Weisner, C.M. 1990. Coercion in Alcohol Treatment. In Institute of Medicine 1990, 579–609.

Wheeler, L. 1990. 66% Polled Say Addiction Should Be Viewed as Illness. *Washinton Post* (11th October), D7.

Whitley, O.R. 1977. Life with Alcoholics Anonymous: The Methodist Class Meeting as a Paradigm. *Journal of Studies on Alcohol*, 38, 831–848.

Wilson, B., and C.G. Jung. 1987. Spiritus Contra Spiritum: The Bill Wilson–C.G. Jung Letters, the Roots of the Society of Alcoholics Anonymous. *Parabola* (Summer), 68–71.

Wilson, W. 1944. Basic Concepts of Alcoholics Anonymous. *Proceedings of the Annual Meeting, Medical Society of the State of New York*.

Winick, C. 1964. The Life Cycle of the Narcotic Addict and of Addiction. *U.N. Bulletin on Narcotics*, 16, 1–11.

Worell, L., and T.N. Tumilty. 1981. The Measurement of Locus of Control among Alcoholics. In Lefcourt 1981, 321–333.

X, Malcolm. 1964. *The Autobiography of Malcolm X*. New York: Ballantine.

Zimmer, L., and J.P. Morgan. 1997. *Marijuana Myths, Marijuana Facts: A Review of the Scientific Evidence*. New York: Lindesmith Center.

Zinberg, N.E., W.M. Hardin, S.M. Stelmack, and R.A. Marblestone. 1978. Patterns of Heroin Use. *Annals of the New York Academy of Science*, 3, 10–24.

Index